THE POWER WITHIN

I know that these principles work. Their miraculous power is not based on a belief, it is a knowing. I know that we have divine power that has gone untapped primarily because of our conditioning. I know that you, if you practice these nine principles studiously, can begin to manifest for yourself virtually anything that you are capable of conceiving in your mind. . . .

Make an effort to read these principles and begin to apply them in your daily life, without judging them based on what you have been conditioned to believe about yourself as a person who is "only human" and, therefore, limited. Preconceptions will only serve to contaminate your unlimited potential for manifesting your heart's desire. What you desire is of central importance, though you may never before have thought of desire and higher spiritual awareness as compatible concepts. . . .

Your desires, cultivated as seeds of potential on the path of spiritual awareness, can blossom in the form of freedom to have these desires in peace and harmony with your world.

Books by Wayne W. Dyer

Your Sacred Self
A Promise Is a Promise
Real Magic
You'll See It When You Believe It
What Do You Really Want for Your Children?
No More Holiday Blues
Gifts from Eykis
The Sky's the Limit
Pulling Your Own Strings
Your Erroneous Zones
Manifest Your Destiny
Wisdom of the Ages
There's a Spiritual Solution to Every Problem

MANIFEST YOUR DESTINY

The Nine Spiritual Principles for
Getting Everything You Want

Wayne W. Dyer

HarperPaperbacks
A Division of HarperCollins*Publishers*

📖 HarperPaperbacks

A Division of HarperCollins*Publishers*

10 East 53rd Street, New York, NY 10022–5299

HarperCollins®, 📖®, and HarperPaperbacks™ are trademarks of
HarperCollins Publishers, Inc.

Cover illustration © 1999 by Richard Rossiter

A hardcover edition of this book was published
in 1997 by HarperCollins*Publishers*.
A trade paperback edition was published
in 1998 by HarperCollins*Publishers*.

First paperback printing: July 1999

Printed in the United States of America

Visit HarperPaperbacks on the World Wide Web at
http://www.harpercollins.com

⌘ 10 9 8 7 6

Monograph

Magnaage

1-800-918-22-8

2999 × 3

Is it not written in your law,
"I have said, You are gods"?

—JOHN, 10:34

On that day, you will know
that I am in my Father,
and you in me,
and I in you.

—JOHN, 14:20

Contents

Y̶ou have the power within you to attract to yourself all that you could ever want. This is the central theme of *Manifest Your Destiny,* which is unlike any book I have previously written. I have chosen to write about this subject of manifesting because I have been drawn to it, rather than because it is the next logical step in the progression of books that I have produced over the past two decades. I seem to have been drawn to the subject by a force that will not allow me to ignore it.

As I began writing, I felt a kind of humility, along with a feeling of arrogance, about taking on this subject matter. These feelings created questions such as: Who am I to write about this capacity to manifest?

What do I really know about manifesting in the first place? Isn't this territory reserved for divine beings? What gives me the authority to tell others about an ability that is unique to the gods? These questions swirled around inside me; I was motivated by more self-doubt than I like to acknowledge.

As I began the task of writing these spiritual principles, I had no idea what I would be saying and how I would say it, nor how many principles were involved. And then I did what I have encouraged my readers to do in my most recent book, *Your Sacred Self.* I banished all my doubts and began listening to the inner voices that kept telling me I would receive the guidance I needed, and that I would not be alone in this project. In other words, I surrendered and went deep within in my meditations and allowed myself to release all fear and doubt and, simply, to trust.

A part of me knew that the ability to manifest into the material world from the unseen world of spirit is possible for all of us. I believed this because the words of all the great spiritual teachers encourage us to see ourselves as unlimited and to know that even the least among us has the divine power of God available at every moment of our lives. But to actually write this in a book, and provide the spiritual principles that one must learn and master in order to do so, seemed a daunting task.

It was at this time, as I was considering writing these principles even though I had no clear idea what they were precisely, and in what order they should be presented, that I received a message from a teacher named Guruji, to whom this book is dedicated. In this message, Shri Guruji instructed me to listen to a tape on the power of manifesting and to practice, in my own life, what I was being taught, and then to present this manifesting technique to the world. He explained that the ability to manifest had been known and practiced by great sages and teachers in the East for thousands of years and has continued in much secrecy for centuries.

I listened with great interest, and began to practice, just as they are presented in this book, the manifestation principles in my daily meditations. I experienced astonishing results almost immediately. I then began to include a discussion of these results in my lectures and to teach these spiritual principles, which I had begun practicing in my life, though without cataloguing or organizing them in any way.

A few months later I produced a compact disc/cassette tape titled *Meditations for Manifesting,* and thousands of people began to use these principles and practice the manifesting meditation techniques. The results have been mind shattering. People who are using these techniques and sound meditations have written to me from all over the world.

The sound meditation, described in this book, has produced amazing manifestations in the lives of many people. I have heard stories of manifesting job promotions, having a baby, which was supposedly an impossibility, selling a home that had been on the market for years without potential buyers, and other stories of prosperity and healing that border on being miracles.

I know that these principles work. Their miraculous power is not based on a belief, it is a knowing. I know that we have divine power that has gone untapped primarily because of our conditioning. I know that *you,* if you practice these nine principles studiously, can begin to manifest for yourself virtually anything that you are capable of conceiving in your mind.

I am aware that entering this realm of manifesting is like walking down an unfamiliar path. When you decide to enter the unknown, you obviously cannot know for sure what is ahead. I ask you, therefore, to avoid cluttering this path with preconceptions. Make an effort to read these principles and begin to apply them in your daily life, without judging them based on what you have been conditioned to believe about yourself as a person who is "only human" and, therefore, limited. Preconceptions will only serve to contaminate your unlimited potential for manifesting your heart's desire. What you desire is of central importance, though you may never before have thought of desire and higher spiritual awareness as compatible concepts.

It is impossible to imagine a world without desire. To create is to desire. Even the wish to be desireless is a desire. The process of creating anything begins first with a desire. Your desires, cultivated as seeds of potential on the path of spiritual awareness, can blossom in the form of the freedom to have these desires in peace and harmony with your world.

Giving yourself permission to explore this path is allowing yourself the freedom to use your mind to create the precise material world that matches your inner world. That inner world is the one which is the catalyst for determining your physical world experiences. You will have to abandon the idea that you are powerless over the circumstances of your life. You will need to shift out of the group mentality that says you are incapable of manifesting. Group thinking inhibits your natural abilities to co-create your life as you desire it to be.

Examine the pressures and beliefs you have bought into, which reflect the thinking of your immediate family, your extended family, your community, your religious grouping, your ethnic grouping, your educational/business grouping or any of a multitude of specialized units of people. Determine the areas of your life that are jammed up with the teachings of those mindsets, causing your personal evolution to be slowed down because what you truly desire or believe is not getting any energy from your unique individuality.

When you stay plugged into group consciousness, you are really saying, "I choose to evolve slowly." Furthermore, that mind-set always gives you permission to be weak and impotent. You choose to evolve with a group rather than spontaneously, as your inner consciousness dictates.

If you truly understand the ability to manifest, you realize you can control the speed at which change occurs in your life. A practicing mystic will manifest quickly because he or she is plugged into the world behind his or her own eyes rather than seeing the world as dictated by the eyes of the group and all of its forebears.

As you experience unplugging your circuits from

those external forces, you will see the speed of your evolvement increase drastically. If you hear a voice behind your eyeballs that says, "Move forward," you no longer wait for everyone else to make a move forward before you take your first step. You no longer have to run your suggestions through the group mind, which is meant to keep you safe and to discourage your individuality.

I was able to begin my journey of enlightenment only when I fully recognized that the group agreement to keep me safe, and to love me *inadequately,* allowed me to seek something of a greater measure. If you wait for everyone else to learn how to manifest their hearts' desires, you will not have enough time in this lifetime to even begin your journey. You must unplug from your conditioning and know in that private space behind your eyes that you can and will take on the challenge of manifesting your destiny.

When you cultivate the inner conviction to manifest from the world of the unseen into the material world, you understand that there is a universal God force that is in all things in the universe. There is not a separate God for each individual, each plant, each animal, each mineral. They are all one. Therefore, the same God force that is within you and causes you to think and breathe is simultaneously in everyone and everything else as well. It is universal. Thus, there is no place that it is not. Consequently, that which you perceive to be missing from your life also contains the same God force or universal intelligence that is within you.

Manifesting, then, becomes the business of doing nothing more than bringing into form a new aspect of yourself. You are not creating something from nothing. You are learning to align yourself with an aspect of your being that your senses have not known they could activate. This is a very important part of this understanding. You and that which you want to manifest into your life are one!

As I wrote this book, I had the most peaceful experience of writing that I have ever enjoyed. What you now hold in your hands is the result of these nine principles. Each day I would do precisely what I have written about in these nine principles.

As I practiced the nine principles, I realized that I was manifesting a handbook for spiritual manifesting that anyone could pick up and begin to apply in the very moments that they were reading the words in this book. I knew that I did not need to fill this book with hundreds of examples of these principles and how they had worked for me and many of my students as well as readers around the world. I knew that it was unnecessary to include a large number of quotes and affirmations as I have done in many of my previous books. This was to be something quite different.

The key word I kept in mind as I wrote and allowed these principles to manifest through me was the word "tight." That meant to me, no extraneous verbiage, no case studies and a minimum of quotations. I was dedicated to a style of writing that I characterized as "Say what you want to say. Say it simply. Say it directly. Say it from your heart and resist any temptation to overwrite." This is what I did in producing this book.

There are no chapters, simply nine principles. Each principle is explained in as straightforward a manner as I know how. Each came directly from my heart and not my head. I listened to my own guidance, and then I wrote it out. When I felt that I had said what was needed to be said, and when I had provided specific suggestions for implementing these principles, I stopped. You are holding in your hand the "tightest" handbook I know how to devise to teach the fundamental principles for spiritual manifestation.

My internal knowing is that when you practice these nine principles you will be given guidance. You will not be alone on this journey, and you will see your desires manifest as your destiny in your daily life.

Finally, you will know that your job is to say "Yes!" rather than "How?" I send you all green lights.

WAYNE W. DYER

BECOMING AWARE OF YOUR HIGHEST SELF

———————————— ☺ ☺ ☺ *The First Principle*

Within you is a divine capacity to manifest and attract all that you need or desire. This is such a powerful statement that I suggest you reread and savor it before you begin this journey.

Most of what we are taught to believe about our reality conflicts with this statement. However, I know it to be so true and valuable that I encourage you to surrender any hesitation and let this thought enter your consciousness: *I have a divine ability to manifest and attract what I need or desire!*

Becoming aware of your highest self does not happen through physical effort, nor can one rely upon supernatural techniques such as invoking angels to do this heavenly work for you. What is essential is that you learn that you are both a physical body in a material world, and a nonphysical being who can gain access to a higher level. That higher level is within you and is reached through the stages of adult development.

The developmental stages of infancy through adolescence have been explored by many writers, but very little has been written about the developmental stages of adulthood. There are four stages that each of us seem to traverse once we reach adulthood. These stages of our lives represent a way of thinking, although they are not necessarily associated with age or experience. Some of us proceed rapidly through these stages, learning at a young age that we are both a physical self and a higher self. Others remain in one of the earlier stages for a lifetime.

Carl Jung, writing in *Modern Man in Search of a Soul,* provided some critical insight into the developmental tasks of adulthood. He believed that an awareness of a higher self is a developmental task of adulthood. In the next section I am offering my interpretation of Dr. Jung's stages of adult development.

I write about these stages with some degree of expertise because I have spent many years in each of them. They have been stepping stones to my awareness of my higher self. Each stage involved experiences that permitted me to move ahead in my thinking and my awareness. Ultimately, I reached the level at which I could use these nine principles to co-create my life. That is, to manifest my own destiny.

As you read these, examine the personal and unique stages of your adult development that parallel

Dr. Jung's archetypes. Your objective is to become aware of your highest self as a dimension of your being that transcends the limitations of the physical world.

THE FOUR STAGES OF ADULT DEVELOPMENT

THE ATHLETE

The word "athlete" is not meant to disparage athletes or athletic behavior. It is intended as a description of the time in our adult lives when our *primary identification* is with our physical body and how it functions in our everyday world. This is the time when we measure our worth and our happiness by our physical appearance and abilities.

Those abilities are multitudinous and uniquely personal. They can include such things as how fast we run, how far we throw a ball, how high we can jump and the size of our muscles. We judge the worthiness of our physical appearance by a standard of attractiveness based on the shape, size, color and texture of body parts, hair and complexion. In a consumer culture like ours, judgment even extends to the appearance of our automobiles, houses and clothes.

These are the concerns one has when he or she is in the earliest stage of adult development. This is the time when life seems impossible without a mirror and a steady stream of approval to make us feel secure. The stage of the athlete is the time in our adult development when we are almost completely identified with our performance, attractiveness and achievements.

Many people outgrow the stage of the athlete and make other considerations more significant. Some of us, depending on our personal circumstances, move in and out of this stage. A few stay in the athlete stage for their entire lives.

Whether or not you have moved beyond the athlete stage is determined by how fixated you are on your body as your primary source of self-identification. Obviously, it is healthy to take good care of your body by treating it kindly and exercising and nourishing it in the best way your circumstances allow. Having pride in your physical appearance and enjoying compliments does not mean you are body-fixated. However, if your daily activities revolve around a predetermined standard of performance and appearance, you are in the stage that I am calling "the athlete."

This is not a stage in which you can practice the art of manifesting. To reach the ability to know and use your divine inner energy, you must move beyond your identification as being exclusively a physical body.

THE WARRIOR

When we leave the athlete stage behind, we generally enter the stage of the warrior. This is the time when the ego dominates our lives and we feel compelled to conquer the world to demonstrate our superiority. My definition of ego is the idea that we have of ourselves as important and separate from everyone else. This can be an acronym for <u>E</u>arth <u>G</u>uide <u>O</u>nly since ego represents our exclusive identification with our physical selves in our material world.

The ego-driven warrior objective is to subdue and defeat others in a race for the number-one spot. During this stage we are busy with goals and achievements in competition with others. This ego-dominated stage is full of anxiety and endless comparison of our success. Trophies, awards, titles and the accumulation of material objects record our achievements. The warrior is intensely concerned with the future and who might be in his way or interfere with his status. He is motivated with slogans such as: "If you don't know where you're going, how will you know when you get there?"; "Time is money, and money is everything"; "Winning isn't everything, it's the only thing"; "Life is a struggle"; "If I don't get mine, someone else will."

In the warrior stage, status and position in life are obsessions. Convincing others of our superiority is the theme of this other-centered time of life in which the ego is the director. This is the time when we are attempting to do what warriors do: conquer and claim the spoils of our battles for ourselves.

The test of whether you have left this stage is to examine what it is that is the driving force in your life. If the answer is conquering, defeating, acquiring, comparing and winning at all costs, then it is clear that you are still in the warrior stage. You can probably regularly shift in and out of the warrior stage as a way of effectively functioning in the marketplace. Only you can determine how intensely that attitude dominates your existence and drives your life. If you do live primarily at this level, you will be unable to become a manifester in the sense that I am describing.

THE STATESPERSON

The statesperson stage of life is the time when we have tamed our ego and shifted our awareness. In this stage we want to know what is important to the other person. Rather than obsessing over our quotas, we can ask what *your* quotas are with genuine interest. We have begun to know that our primary purpose is to give rather than to get. The statesperson is still an achiever and quite often athletic. However, the inner drive is to serve others.

Authentic freedom cannot be experienced until one learns to tame the ego and move out of self-absorption. When you find yourself upset, anxious or feeling off purpose, ask yourself how much of your emotional state has to do with your assessment of how you are being treated and perceived. When you can let go of your own thoughts about yourself and not think of yourself for a long period of time, that is when you are free.

Shifting out of the warrior stage and into the statesperson stage of life was an extremely freeing experience for me. Before I made the shift I had to consider all of my ego needs when I gave a public lecture. This meant worrisome thoughts about how I would be received and reviewed, whether people would want to purchase my books and tapes, or fears about losing my place and becoming embarrassed.

Then came a time when, without any concerted effort, I began to meditate before my lectures. During my meditation I would silently recite a mantra asking how I might serve. My speaking improved significantly when I shifted away from my ego and entered the stage of statesperson.

The statesperson stage of adulthood is about service and gratefulness for all that shows up in your life. At this level you are very close to your highest self. The primary force in your life is no longer the desire to be the most powerful and attractive or to dominate and conquer. You have entered the realm of inner peace. It is always in the service of others, regardless of what you do or what your interests are, that you find the bliss you are seeking.

One of the most touching stories I have ever heard is of Mother Teresa, who even in her eighties ministers to the downtrodden in the streets of Calcutta. A friend of mine in Phoenix was scheduled to do a radio interview with her. As they spoke before the interview, Pat said to her, "Mother Teresa, is there anything I can do to help you with your cause? Could I help you raise money or give you some publicity?"

Mother Teresa replied, "No, Pat, there is nothing that you need do. My cause is not about publicity, and it is not about money. It is about something much higher than that."

Pat persisted, saying, "Isn't there anything I can do for you? I feel so helpless."

Mother Teresa's response was, "If you really want to do something, Pat, tomorrow morning get up at four A.M. and go out on the streets of Phoenix. Find someone living there who believes that he is alone, and convince him that he is not. That is what you can do." This is a true statesperson, giving of herself each and every day.

When we help others to know that they are not alone, that they too have a divine spirit within them regardless of the circumstances of their lives, we move to a higher self that provides us with a sense of peace and purpose unavailable in the athlete and warrior experiences. It is here that we might recall the words of Mother Teresa: "I see Jesus Christ every day in all of his distressing disguises."

There is one stage even higher than the statesperson. The fourth stage is where I have been carefully leading you on this journey of awareness development.

THE SPIRIT

When you enter this stage of life, regardless of your age or position, you recognize your truest essence, the highest self. When you know your highest self, you are on your way to becoming a co-creator of your entire world, learning to manage the circumstances of your life and participating with assurance in the act of creation. You literally become a manifester.

The spirit stage of life is characterized by an awareness that this place called earth is not your home. You know that you are not an athlete, a warrior, or even a statesperson, but that you are an infinite, limitless, immortal, universal and eternal energy temporarily residing in a body. You know that nothing dies, that everything is an energy that is constantly changing.

As a soul with a body you are passionately drawn to your inner world. You leave fears behind and start to experience a kind of detachment from this physical plane. You become an observer of your world and you move into other dimensions of consciousness. This inner infinite energy is not just in you, it is in all things and all people who are alive now and have ever lived. You begin to know this intimately.

In order to evolve beyond the earth plane, you need to learn to leave it at will by finding the source of this infinite energy that is responsible for filling your lungs, beating your heart, growing your hair and making it possible for you to read the words on this page. You the physical being are not growing your hair, your nature is doing that for you. The energy that is you is handling all of the details. That spirit that is you is not contained by the physical domain at all. It has no boundaries, no form, no limits to its outer edges. You are aware of the real source of your life, even though you have been conditioned to believe otherwise.

When you reach this level, you are in the space I think of as *being in this world, but not of this world.*

This energy that is you, call it what you will—spirit, soul—can never die and has never died in the past. Most people think of the spiritual world as a future occurrence that they will know after death. Most of us have been taught that the highest self is something that you cannot know as long as you are trapped in a body on this planet. However, the spirit is now. It is in you in this moment, and the energy is not something that you will ultimately come to know but is what you are here and now.

The unseen energy that was once in Shakespeare or Picasso or Galileo, or any human form, is also available to all of us. That is because the spirit energy does not die, it simply changes form.

Even though our rational left-brain mind has been trained to believe that when a person dies his spirit is gone, the truth is that you cannot destroy energy. Your highest self is the spirit presently within you. The energy that was Picasso was not his body, nor was the energy that was Shakespeare his body. It was the inner feelings and the creative genius that took the form of a body and a creation on canvas or paper. That has never died. It can't die because it has no boundaries, no beginning, no end, no physical characteristics that we call form.

That energy is within you. If you want to know it, you can tune into it, and when you do, you leave the limitations of this earth plane and enter a dimension of limitlessness that allows you to create and attract to you whatever it is that you want or need on this journey.

At this level you loosen your emotional attachment to what you view as your reality. This detachment is followed by a knowing that the observer within you who is always noticing your surroundings and your thoughts is in reality the source of your physical world.

This awareness, along with your willingness to enter this domain, is the beginning of learning to attract to yourself that which you desire and need while you are in a physical body.

Up to this point, you probably have been unable to loosen your attachment to the material world. You may believe that there is no other world. If so, you have actually abandoned your divine capability, which is the cause of the sensory world you so assiduously embrace. Gaining the awareness that you have a higher self that is universal and eternal will lead you to gaining access to that world more freely and to participating in the act of manifesting your heart's desire.

THE SEEN AND THE UNSEEN

Consider for a moment the world of form that you see around you, including your body. What is the cause of all that you observe? Contemplate who it is that observes and notices all of the "stuff." Who is that invisible "I" inside all of the tubes, bones, arteries and skin that are your physical form? To know yourself authentically, you must understand that everything that you notice around you was and is caused by something in the world of the unseen. That something is the world of the spirit.

When you look at a giant oak tree, ask yourself what caused that tree to become what it is. It started from a tiny acorn, a seedling that grew into a mighty tree. Your logical, rational mind says that there must be something resembling "treeness" within that acorn. But when you open the acorn you find nothing resembling a tree. All you find is a mass of brown stuff, quiet dust. If you further examine the brown stuff that makes up the acorn, you will find smaller shreds of brown stuff, until ultimately you discover distinctly "acornish" molecules. Then you find atoms, then electrons, then subatomic particles, until you finally go as small as is possible with a microscope at full magnification. Here you will find that there are no particles, but waves of energy that mysteriously come and go.

Your conclusion will be that the acorn and the tree itself have a creator that is unseen, immeasurable and called by those of us who need to classify such things the spirit or soul. The source of all therefore is nothing, since it is not in the dimension of the measurable.

This unseen world that is the source of the world of the seen is also the cause of you. Observe yourself scientifically and you will discover that you are not your creation. If you did not create yourself, what was it that created you?

We can go back to conception and explain creation as one drop of human protoplasm colliding with another, resulting in your appearance in the form of a tiny speck that grew into the body that is you today. But, if you delve further into those drops of human protoplasm and turn up the magnification on the microscope, and if you do the same with the speck that was your first experience of form, you discover the same truth that described the acorn. In the beginning is energy, energy that has no dimensions, energy that is not in the visible world. This is our original self. It is a potentiality, not an object. A "future pull," if you will, that is a potential to become a something and no-thing more.

The general concept of soul or spirit is that you have one, but it is not that important to daily life. It may become really significant, though, after your body dies. I am taking a different position here, and it is the core of this first principle of manifesting. It will lead you to your highest self, and then on to the ability to live a miraculous life of co-creating with God your ideal state of being. Furthermore, this spirit is permanent and incapable of being lost or removed.

Your destiny is to become a co-creator with God and to treasure the sanctity of all that comes into this world of form that we call home, but which is only a transitory stopping place.

Your creative ability originates in the unseen mind. It begins in the unseen world of waves and energy. So, too, do the planets, the stars, the flowers, the animals, the rocks, you, your possessions, your creations—all of it, no exceptions. Examine everything and anything and you find that at the core there is no form, only an unseen quality that brings it from the world of the unseen to the world of the observable.

It is this world of the unseen that I would like you to consider as you read these words. Imagine that there are two worlds in which you co-exist at all times. Look around you now at the world of form. Then look within and realize that it began in the

unseen dimension that we are not even close to com-
prehending.

Then, make the big leap to the awareness that you
are both of these worlds simultaneously. You are not
separate from the world of the unseen any more than
you could be separate from the world of the seen. You
are a combination of both at all moments of your life,
even if you have come to believe that you reside exclusively in the world of the seen, and that the unseen is
something other than you. It is you, all of it. Right
now!

The problem that faces most of us in becoming manifesters and learning to manage the circumstances of our
lives is that we have forfeited our ability to oscillate
between the world of form and the unseen world. Imagine that there is a line down the middle of the room that
you are in at this moment. Pretend that everything to
the right of the line represents the world of the seen. To
the left of the line is everything that is the cause of
everything on the right. The unseen world is on the left,
the seen world is on the right.

Now, question your belief that you (the whole you)
cannot enter the world to the left of the imaginary
line. If you were to cross that line every now and then,
you would be entering the world of the creator. Have
you been taught that the creator is something outside yourself? (I will deal with this more thoroughly in
the second principle.) If so, your inner world (the
world of the unseen) is full of notions that prohibit you
from participating in the creative process.

There are dogmas that represent participating in

the creative process as blasphemy, or foolishness, or thinking too highly of yourself. But go back to the opening sentence of this first principle and reread it until it resonates within you: *Within you is a divine capacity to manifest and attract all that you need or desire.*

It is more than within you. It *is* you, and you must overcome your conditioning and give yourself permission to enter this world. Cross the line that separates the physical you from the you that is just as real, but unseen. When you overcome the obstacles of your mind that prevent you from crossing the line, your unseen self will be your ticket to creation in your life.

TRANSCENDING YOUR CONDITIONING

Like it or not, all of us have been conditioned to think and act in ways that have become automatic. We need to figure out how to get past this conditioning if we want to gain access to our highest self. You can be sure the ego will not take well to this kind of effort.

Asking the ego to help diminish its own significance so that you might have access to your higher self is akin to attempting to stand on your own shoulders. Ego is as unable to move aside in deference to spirit as your eye is able to see itself or the tip of your tongue able to touch the tip of your tongue!

Your task thus becomes a quagmire of paradoxes. If you rely upon your ego to get past the influences of the ego, it will only strengthen its hold on you. You must figure out how to emancipate consciousness from the limitations of your mind and your body.

In the ego state you generally experience yourself as a separate entity. To move past this conditioning you want to begin to see yourself as humanity itself rather than as a separate form in a body. Very simply put, if you feel that you are disconnected from the rest of humanity and truly a separate entity needing to prove yourself and compete with others, you will be unable to manifest your heart's desire.

Manifesting is not about getting things that are not here. It is about attracting what is already here and is a part of you on a spiritual level. If you remain separate, that which you wish to manifest will forever be unavailable to you. If you shift that awareness around and are able to see yourself as a part of what you desire, you will have transcended the conditioning of your ego, and of all the other egos who have contributed to this process in your life.

With the realization of God within yourself, you not only dissolve your ego's identification as separate from God, but you leave behind the old ways of seeing yourself. As you awaken to your highest self, your conditioning as a separate being will be overcome with practice.

Below are a few of the conditioned thoughts that will keep your ego in charge of your life and prevent you from materializing what you desire and what desires you.

1: *I am not in charge of my life. That force is outside me.*
   This kind of conditioned response to the circum-

stances of your life puts the responsibility on something outside you and becomes a handy excuse when your life is not going as you would like it to.

You can change this perception in any given moment, and begin to trust that the vital force of the universe is exactly what you are. Entertain this notion every day by noticing the life force flowing through you. Turn your attention away from the ego-dominated thoughts *about* the circumstances of your life to the present moment by consciously noticing your breath, the sounds, textures, smells and scenes that the life force is experiencing through you. Practice stepping away from the thoughts about your life in any given moment, and step into the *experience* of the life energy flowing through your senses.

2: *People cannot manifest, it is all a function of the cosmic throw of the dice.* This is a very popular idea, particularly for those who are in less than propitious circumstances. Blaming luck or some external, invisible force that controls the universe is a habit of conditioning that leads to disempowerment and, ultimately, defeat. You will have to rid yourself of this hallucination that you are powerless to attract what you desire. Keep in mind that you are not playing magic when you learn to manifest, you are simply manifesting a new aspect of yourself that has been hidden.

You are the universe. It is not something out-

side you. You are that force which is in everything,
even the things that have previously failed to show
up in your life. Remember, as you think, so shall
you be. If you think you can't, you are right, and
that is precisely what you will see showing up in
your life. The results of "I can't" lead to the next
conditioned response.

3: *I have tried before and it has never worked for me.*
Here, the conditioned response is believing that
once having tried and failed, further efforts will
yield the same results. A key word in this
thought is "try." Trying means struggling, working at it, giving it a lot of effort, setting goals and
so forth.

Just for a moment, stop and try to pick up a
pencil from the table. Just try to pick it up. You
will find that there is no such thing as trying. You
either pick it up or you don't. Period. What you
call trying to pick it up is simply not picking up
the pencil.

Let go of your obsession with the past and with
trying, and instead remain relaxed and casual and
in the moment, noticing your life force minus
your judgments and explanations. You will see
good multiply as needed, when you come to know
that you are not powerless to make it happen. The
universe is rich with abundance that will be provided to you when you let go of reasoning that says
your past must be your present.

The reason that you have been unsuccessful in

manifesting what you want is because you are attached to an idea that is erroneous. Your past is an illusion. It is the trail left behind you, and a trail behind you cannot drive you today, regardless of what you choose to believe. All you have is now, and you have never tried anything. You have simply not done it yet. You can now shift that reasoning right out of your inner world.

4: *Only highly evolved beings can manifest.* This is the ego saying that you are separate and distinct from your spiritual teachers and others who live at the highest levels. Even though every spiritual practice encourages you to see the divine within yourself, to know you have in you the same mind as your master, and to discover the kingdom of heaven within yourself, your ego cannot buy it. It is sold on separateness, and convinces you that you are less than those highly evolved beings you've heard about.

Relinquish those thoughts and replace them with seeing yourself as connected to everyone by that unseen life force that is your divine essence. Refuse to put others either above or below you, but instead see them as you. It is necessary to grasp this idea firmly before you can experience true manifestation.

These are a few of the thoughts that swirl around in your head whenever you contemplate the idea of having what you want and need want and need you.

This first spiritual principle directs you to overcome your conditioning. It requires you to adopt a new attitude about yourself, and then to put this attitude into daily practice. I am encouraging you to know the highest self rather than read about it. To know it in the deepest reaches of your being, and then to never again doubt it.

Having a philosophy is useless if it is simply an awareness of rituals and the teachings of experts. To make your philosophy work for you it must become an energy pattern that you use in your daily life. It must have both an eternal truth to it as well as a utilitarian quality that makes you feel, yes, I know this to be true because I apply it and it works.

You do have a highest self. You can know this highest self in both the seen and the unseen dimensions of your life. Once you are convinced of this, the belief that the ego is the dominant motivating force in your life will lose its power.

I encourage you to follow these suggestions for developing this first principle as a permanent part of your total awareness. This plan of action worked for me. If I encounter doubt, I return to this four-point plan. It always reacquaints me with the highest self.

HOW TO KNOW YOUR HIGHEST SELF WITHOUT ANY DOUBT

1: *Here is a great definition of enlightenment: to be immersed in and surrounded by peace.* Your highest self only wants you to be at peace. It does not judge, compare or demand that you defeat anyone, or be better than anyone. It only wants you to be at peace. Whenever you are about to act, ask yourself this question: "Is what I am about to say or do going to bring me peace?" If the answer is yes, then go with it and you will be allowing yourself the wisdom of your highest self. If the answer is no, then remind yourself that it is your ego at work.

The ego promotes turmoil because it wants to substantiate your separateness from everyone, including God. It will push you in the direction of judgment and comparison, and cause you to insist on being right and best. You know your highest self by listening to the voice that only wants you to be at peace.

2: *Go beyond the restriction of the physical plane.* The purpose of the highest self is to assist you in this effort. You do this by creating an inner sanctuary that is yours and yours alone. Go to this silent inner retreat as often as you can, and let go of all attachments to the external world of the ego.

As you go to this sanctuary, a light will be born within you that you will come to know and respect. This light is your connection to the energy of manifestation. It is like taking a bath in pure light; you will feel this energy as you go silently within. This light is not of the earth plane. It will help you go beyond the physical world.

Remember, you cannot go beyond the earth plane if you are still in it. The real you, the unseen you, can attract the energy of the sun, the wind and all that is celestial.

3: *Refuse to defend yourself to anyone or anything on the earth plane.* You must learn to stay within your higher energy pattern regardless of what goes before you in the material world. This means that you become like an unknown sage who refuses to lock horns with anything on this physical plane.

This is the challenge of the highest self. It is beyond the reality system that you identify as material and as form. Use your inner light for your alignment and allow those who disagree with that perspective to have their own points of view. You are at peace. You never explain, and you refuse to flaunt your energy. You know it, and that is enough for you.

4: *Finally, surrender and trust in the wisdom that created you.* You are developing a faith that transcends the beliefs and teachings of others. This trust is your corner of freedom, and it will always be yours. In fact, it is so important that it is the subject of the second spiritual principle of manifestation, which you will read about when you turn to the next section.

☉ ☉ ☉

Your highest self is not just an idea that sounds lofty and spiritual. It is a way of being. It is the very first principle that you must come to understand and embrace as you move toward attracting to you that which you want and need for this parenthesis in eternity that you know as your life.

TRUSTING YOURSELF IS TRUSTING THE WISDOM THAT CREATED YOU

——————— ☽ ☽ ☽ *The Second Principle*

*L*earning to trust may be difficult in the beginning. It will be an exercise in futility if you rely upon your mind to create trust. This is because the mind works on material problems by interpreting sensory data. When turned toward spiritual matters the mind attempts to come up with intellectual answers by using proofs, logic and theoretical reasoning. It demands assurance and proof to establish tangible results.

In contrast, the method of the heart, focused on spiritual understanding, is an intuitive recognition of the value of love. Whereas the mind attempts to know the spirit by setting up conditions that must be met logically for there to be a release of love, the heart employs intuitive love as its way. It is not a conclusion of reasoning. It is the way of spontaneity, not the result of bargaining with the intellect. The heart trusts the inner wisdom that it feels and spontaneously knows, whereas the mind demands scientific evidence before it will trust.

Most of us in the West have been taught that the center of our wisdom is in our heads. If you ask people where their ability to process thought and experience is, they will generally respond that it is in the brain. Ask consciously spiritual persons the same question and they will indicate the heart.

When the mind seeks corroboration through specific proofs as an aid to spiritual understanding, it is encroaching into an area far more suited to the heart. For this reason, it is necessary to trust what the heart knows. Without total trust, it is impossible to know the miracles of the higher self and become a manifester.

Spiritual life does not grow in the soil of intellectual information gathering. Spirituality needs the fertile ground of feelings, which the unseen dimension provides. Trusting your heart space is imperative for the growth of a healthy spiritual life.

This means cultivating a harmony between mind and heart, and for most of us this means terminating the intellect's domination. The mind must surrender its role as full-time judge and allow the heart to contribute its wisdom. It is with this surrendering process that trust begins to flourish, replacing doubt.

Mistrust begins early in most human beings' lives. It is helpful to realize why it is that the heart space has not been permitted to be the center of our being. Here are two theories describing our place in nature. I think you will agree that the first theory illuminates why mistrust of ourselves and our divine abilities is so deeply rooted.

TWO THEORIES OF NATURE THAT AFFECT OUR ABILITY TO TRUST

First Theory: Nature as a Mechanism

In the mechanistic view of nature, everything is an artifact made by a boss who has many different names. In the Western view, the boss is called God.

This God is often depicted as a white-bearded male who roams around the sky creating the natural world. In this theory, the world is a construct and God the constructor. This biblical God is paternal, authoritarian, beneficent and, in many ways, tyrannical. He keeps track of all things and knows precisely what everyone does and when his laws are being broken.

One of the operatives of this theory of nature is the idea of punishment for one's sins. This God/father holds us accountable for transgressions. The transgressions are judged by various interpreters of his laws who throughout history have claimed access to the divine. Essentially, the universe is a monarchy, God the king and we the subjects. All subjects are considered born with the stain of sin as a part of their nature and are therefore untrustworthy.

This theory of nature makes many people feel

estranged, creating an attitude of separateness from the boss. The more we feel separated from this God, the more we feel the need to create some way of feeling worthy. So we create an idea of our importance based on externals and call it "ego."

Reliance on ego ultimately leads to more separation as life becomes a contest and a competition with designated others. But the sense of estrangement is partially assuaged with an ego-directed attitude of "us against them." People are categorized and evaluated on the basis of "egonomics," which includes appearance, tradition, language and physical characteristics.

I believe that the most troubling thing built into this theory of nature is the impact it has on our ability to operate from a strong position of self-trust. Once convinced that you are untrustworthy and basically a sinner, you are quite lost. If you are untrustworthy, how can you trust in even your untrustworthiness? You can't!

Everything becomes subject to doubt when God is a vindictive boss. This leads to the confusion of doubting everything because our opinions, feelings and beliefs are untrustworthy. In this scenario, one cannot even maintain trust in God because of a basic mistrust of ourselves. And not trusting in that God may be breaking one of his laws. It is a no-win situation.

This theory of the untrustworthiness of nature, popular as it is, is absolutely incompatible with the second principle of manifestation. You cannot tune into the power and energy of the universe to create and attract an abundant life if that energy and power is outside you.

Second Theory: Nature as Spontaneous and Nonjudging

In this spontaneous view, God is universal intelligence flowing through everything, inspiring the natural process to unfold. The emphasis is on awareness of the divine nature in everything rather than managing and controlling the natural world. The life force is nonjudgmental and is responsible for all creation.

In this theory, nature is an unforced unfolding of life forms and there is no "boss." Rather than learning to manage and control the natural world, the impulse is to trust it. God, in this theory, loves all things.

Human beings are an aspect of this God and are, therefore, carriers of divinity. Generally, in this theory, human beings are considered the highest level of life form. Trusting this most evolved natural human includes trusting the paradox of behavior described as good and bad, selfish and unselfish, greedy and generous in the same manner as we respect other life forms by trusting their processes.

There is no need to invent an ego that is separate from the divine if our basic human nature is trusted. If we trust ourselves, we know how to avoid interfering with nature and how to live in harmony. When we know God as an unseen, loving and accepting power at the heart of everything, allowing us to make our own choices, then God is a trusted part of our nature.

I believe that our nature is much more reliable than our thoughts. This second principle directs us to develop an inner knowing so that the natural process of what we desire also desires us. Consider how our biological system attracts what is needed for hair to grow, food to digest, fingernails to be hard or breasts to be soft without our thoughts directing the process. Thinking can often lead us astray, while our nature unfolds in the form of amazingly well-functioning bodies and minds. When you trust this natural process, you begin to trust the nature of all things. The God within all informs your trusting response to life.

The order of nature itself is sometimes crooked and sometimes straight. It is wiggly and unorthodox, as seen in the shapes of clouds or mountains. They are not in any pattern that we can perceive, and they are perfect. When we insist on controlling nature, we are interfering with nature.

The need to straighten out nature shows distrust. But when we relax and embrace the infinite variations of the universe, we are allowing the divinity of nature to flow and unfold through our life. We have tuned in to the divine.

Think of yourself as a consciousness being played out by God just as a wave is a part of the ocean that is being played out by the ocean. This theory of nature will promote the kind of trust that you need to attract to yourself all that belongs to you in the universe. This unseen, divine energy is the ocean that your wave form is a part of. You can call it God, ocean or, for that matter, anything else.

This is a profoundly exquisite realization because with it you bring to your consciousness the inner awareness that you are actually in all things. This leads to miraculous manifestations, in that you are actually connected to all that you desire to manifest, and finally you know this to be your truth.

BEING IN ALL THINGS AT ONCE

Authentic trust is only available through the knowing heart. When you enter this trusting space, everything will come to you that belongs to you because you have created the inner capacity to receive it. The irony is that what you wish to receive is a part of you. This can be a troublesome concept to grasp because of the ego's attachment to being separate and special.

Nothing in your rational mind could ever convince you that water is made of two parts hydrogen and one part oxygen. It appears to be a fluid that flows and has nothing to do with gases. But when we subject water to scrutiny, its constituent elements become manifest. And so it is with the idea of being in all things at once.

Nothing in our everyday experience gives us much reason to believe that our mind has as one of its constituents something invisible that is in all living things. Yet when we examine our life force, using quantum mechanics, we find that this energy is, indeed, not a particle but a wave that is the same in all life.

You trust in the universal energy when you accept this "irrational" fact: At your basic core you are not only worthy of trust, but you are the life force that exists everywhere. If you truly trust in this notion, you realize that everything that you perceive as missing in your life is a part of the same energy that you are. Manifesting becomes the art of bringing to yourself that which is already you.

In a sense it is like thinking of the things you want as being on a string that is infinitely long, but is nevertheless attached to you in some invisible way. It is only a matter of trusting that you can bring that string to you and that whatever is supposed to come to your life will be there when you have developed the capacity to receive it. But the trick is, you cannot receive it or even come close to manifesting it if you have an absence of trust in yourself as an extension of God.

I like to think of God as the ocean and myself as a glass. If I dip the glass into the ocean, I will have a glass full of God. No matter how I analyze this, it will still contain God. Now, the glass of God is not as big as the ocean, nor is it omniscient or omnipotent, but it is still God. This metaphor allows me to trust both in myself and simultaneously in the wisdom that created me, and to see the oneness.

I have deliberately chosen not to use many quotations in this book. But I want to emphasize that every spiritual master and all of the saints, teachers, gurus or priests throughout history have espoused similar advice. This perennial philosophy connects all humanity, from tribal and ancient to civilized and present times. It is the message that God is within and outside every living thing. Also, there is a world we are a part of that is not subject to the changing world of time and space. Moreover, we are presently a part of that invisible spiritual world.

Since it is everywhere, it is not only within you, it *is*

you. The meaning of this is that God is not to be found
so much as discovered within yourself. The statement
"You and the Father are one" is more than an ecclesi-
astical admonition. It is a statement of your reality.

With practice, you can learn to know this reality. You
can learn to see the aura around all living things. You can
learn to assist others by projecting your energy and giving them strength and sustenance. Actually, it is not a
skill to learn so much as it is trusting the energy to be
part of you.

It may be that the most effective way to trust your
reality is through the power of prayer. Prayer and trust
offer us seemingly magical methods for manifesting
the divine desire. But, first you may have to shift old
perceptions concerning prayer and discover a whole
new inner vision about praying and prayer.

PRAYER AND TRUST

In the matter of prayer it seems that we often view
God as a gigantic vending machine in the sky who will
grant us our wishes when we put in the proper tokens
in the form of prayers. We expect to insert prayers,
then pull on the knob and hope that God will dispense
the goodies. The God vending machine becomes the
object of our veneration. We tell the machine how
good it is and how much we worship it and expect it to
be good to us in return.

The basic premise here is that God is outside us and
therefore what we need and want is also outside us.
This form of prayer is like practicing the absence

rather than the presence of God. If we believe that we are separate from God, the vending machine approach to prayer reinforces and deepens that belief.

I prefer to promote the idea of prayer in its essence as a communion with God. Praying at the spiritual level then becomes communing with and knowing that God is as close as our breath. What we seek in prayer is the experience of co-existing with God. Prayer is our communication of readiness for the desires of this sacred energy to manifest through our human form. No separation, no absence of God within, simply the presence of this force within ourselves.

Therefore, the true experience of God does not change or alter God, but it changes us. It heals our sense of separation. If we are not changed by prayer, we have denied ourselves the opportunity to know the wisdom that created us.

The search for happiness outside ourselves rekindles an idea that we are not whole and relegates prayer to the status of a plea to a boss/God. We are then asking for favors rather than seeking a manifestation of our invisible, inspired self.

Prayer, at the spiritual level I am writing about, is not asking for something any more than the attempt to become a manifester is asking for something to show up in your life. What I call authentic prayer is inviting divine desire to express itself through me. It is a prayer for what it is that is for my highest purpose and good, or for the greater benefit of all mankind. Prayer at this level expresses my experience of oneness with the divine energy.

This may sound like a radical or even blasphemous notion to you, but it is the source of all spiritual traditions. Here are a few examples.

Christianity: The kingdom of heaven is within you.

Islam: Those who know themselves know their God.

Buddhism: Look within, you are the Buddha.

Vedanta (part of Hinduism): Atman (individual consciousness) and Brahman (universal consciousness) are one.

Yoga (part of Hinduism): God dwells within you as you.

Confucianism: Heaven, earth and human are of one body.

Upanishads (part of Hinduism): By understanding the self, all this universe is known.

Overcoming your conditioning in this area is crucially important. At first, you may be able to accept this idea on an intellectual level, but be unable to make it your authentic experience. So, I suggest you make prayer your experience by using it to replace the random, continuous thoughts that you have all day. Use your trust to commune with God rather than to be in a constant state of chatter.

Replace thoughts *about* your experiences with the

experience of prayer. For instance, praying in this sense can be a sentence such as "Sacredness guide me now" or "Sacred love flow through me now" silently recited instead of thinking thoughts. Prayer in this form is tilling and clearing the inner self of ego chatter so that what you desire and what desires you can grow. My personal practice of prayer is participating in a communion with God wherein I see God within me and ask for the strength and the inner awareness to handle whatever confronts me. I know that I am not separate from this vital force that we call God. I know that this force connects me to everything in the universe and that by placing my attention on what it is that I want to attract to myself I am really doing nothing more than manifesting a new aspect of myself.

I then let go of the results and let the universe handle the details. I retreat in peace and keep reminding myself that heaven on earth is a choice that I must make, not a place I must find. It is my choice to live with the God force flowing unrestricted through me, and it is the way of co-creating my life at this moment. Trust, then, is the cornerstone of my praying, and with it comes the peace that is the essence of manifesting.

PEACE: THE RESULT OF TRUST

The highest self wants you to experience peace, which is a definition of enlightenment. You may recall that I wrote earlier in this book that I define enlightenment as being immersed in and surrounded by peace. The more you trust in the wisdom that creates all, the more you will be trusting in yourself. The result of trusting is that an enormous sense of peace becomes available to you.

When the ego insists on winning, comparing or judging, you will be able to soothe and calm the ego's fears with the peacefulness born of trust. When you are able to trust, you know that God and you are one, like the glass of ocean water and the ocean itself. You are what the God force is doing, just as a wave is what the ocean is doing.

As this awareness grows you will discover that you are a more peaceful person and, consequently, that enlightenment becomes the way of your life. Being independent of the good opinion of others and being detached from the need to be right are two powerful indicators that your life is shifting toward a consciousness of trust in yourself and trust in God. Yet there are many people in our lives who disturb our state of peacefulness. Then, the question is how to handle those who consciously or unconsciously disturb our experience of trust and peace.

I once wrote an essay in a somewhat facetious tone titled "Your Soulmate Is the Person You Can Hardly Stand." The essence of the essay was that the people in our lives who we agree with and share similar interests with are easy to accept and actually teach us very little. But those who can push our buttons and send us into a rage at the slightest provocation are our real teachers.

The person who is most capable of disturbing your state of peace is a person who is reminding you that you are not truly in the state of peace or enlightenment that results from trust. At that moment, this person is your greatest teacher. This is the person whom you want to treasure and thank God for sending into your life! When you can transcend the rage, anger and upset which that person appears to provoke, and instead say, "Thank you for being my teacher," you have acknowledged a soulmate relationship.

Everyone in your life who can still push your buttons and send you into that frenzied state is a master teacher disguised as a manipulative, inconsiderate, frustrating, non-understanding being. The peace that is enlightenment means that you are not only at peace with those who share your interests and agree with you, and with strangers who come and go, but also with those master teachers who remind you that you still have some work to do on yourself.

Give thanks for those great spiritual masters who have arrived in your life in the form of your children, current or former spouses, irritating neighbors, co-workers, obnoxious strangers and the like, for they help you stay in an enlightened, peaceful state. They let you know each day how much more work you truly have to do and in what ways you have not mastered yourself.

Peace occurs when your highest self is dominant in your life. When you begin to feel peace as the result of trust, you are enjoying a healthy soul. Keep in mind that there is only one real soul, and that your personality is a vehicle for the whole. You cannot divide the infinite. There is no division. You must trust this awareness.

When you divide, you have moved out of identification with the God force and have taken up shelter in the ego. It is here that you will find an absence of peace and also an absence of trust in the wisdom that created you.

There are many things that you can do on a regular basis to make this second principle of trusting in the oneness a reality in your life. Here are a few suggestions to nurture trust in yourself and in the oneness.

HOW TO TRUST IN YOURSELF AND THE WISDOM THAT CREATED YOU

- Begin by admitting your confusion or failures. When you do this, you are dismissing any illusion of trust, which is in reality a false self-trust. Remind yourself that genuine trust involves letting go of all conditioning that teaches you that trust in yourself is based on being special or separate.

  When you are honest with yourself about every aspect of your life, you discontinue identifying with separateness. You then become ready for the insight that trust in yourself and trust in ultimate truth are one and the same. Remind yourself often that you are a child of God and that you have the God force within you. Let the statements "I am it" and "It is me" rise from your inner being.

- Keep in mind that you cannot go to a higher ground if you are hanging onto a lower level. You cannot leave the physical world if you are so attached to it that you refuse to let go. The concept of trust involves surrendering and trusting the God force.

Imagine yourself falling from a precipice while clinging to a huge rock, believing that it will protect you. Letting go of the rock is a metaphor for surrendering and trusting. You will continue to live and breathe in the physical earth plane, but you realize that you are not only your body and mind, and that the rock is not your salvation. Your needs and demands cease, and you are one with the manifest consciousness.

Of course, you are literally still in the body, but you have also joined the manifest consciousness. This trust allows you to participate in the act of creation. Your current world will be experienced anew. The freedom and respect you receive from God will be bestowed by you on the circumstances of your world.

① Acquire a rebellious attitude toward the philosophy that preaches a style of God-as-boss who is authoritarian and a benevolent tyrant. Rejection of this model does not mean that you are an atheist, but rather a believer in the true meaning of divinity.

You are not required to feel inferior, to view yourself as a sinner and to prostrate yourself before idols and dogma in order to believe in God. Study St. Paul in the New Testament where he says, "Let this mind be in you, which was also in Christ Jesus: Who being in the form of God, thought it not robbery to be equal with God." This is the kind of trust you must adopt in order to know your divine self.

⊙ Trusting does not mean you never experience life's valleys. There will be peaks and valleys as long as you live on this physical plane. There is no happiness without the opposite experience of unhappiness. Opposites are the way it is in the physical plane. Expect that this is also your reality.

Do not abandon trust when your ego thinks things should be different than they are. It is better to embrace trust when darkness is present, knowing that light will follow. Begin to look for the lesson in the darkness rather than cursing it. Trust allows you simply to observe the dark and unhappy times rather than identifying totally with those aspects of life. From this perspective you are not at the mercy of your ego energy, insisting that everything must be perfect, and that when things are not, you have reasons to give up your trust in the divine.

The valleys are merely the way of the physical plane, but they are not who you are. You are part of the unseen wisdom that created this entire physical plane and you can trust in it uncategorically.

⊙ There is timeless wisdom in this old idea of trust. Any person can sense that problems are within, but the spiritually trusting person realizes that the solution is also within.

When you trust in yourself, you are not looking for solutions to your life problems in someone or something outside yourself. Instead, you remain in a state of trusting. Then, in a trustworthy manner, you can proceed to attract the energy to you that provides the solution.

⏲ Take your most serious problems and turn them over to God. Say something like the following: "I have not been able to resolve these issues in my life and I have used every technique I know. I would like to show my trust in the divine force by simply turning them over to your divine hands. As I do this I know that the divine force that is you, God, is also me, and I trust that this action will lead to a resolution of these problems."

I can assure you that this method puts you into direct contact with a higher power than can ever be found in a bottle, a bank statement, a contrary partner, an illness or anything on the earth plane that you believe is external or separate from you. I left all of the addictions of my life behind me with the simple words "I've tried everything else, now I am trusting God."

It was not as though something outside myself was now doing it for me. I simply trusted that force, and it began showing up in my daily abstinence program. I trusted in the eternal wisdom and I also trusted in myself to receive that wisdom and apply it. This same process has been the source of all of the manifesting that has occurred and continues to transpire in my daily life.

☉ The presence of complete trust is evident in your life when what you think, feel and do are all balanced and in harmony. The presence of a distinction between your thoughts and your emotional state as well as your behavior tends to move you away from the trusting attitude I am encouraging you to adopt as you practice this second principle of manifestation.

Examine your thoughts carefully. See if those thoughts are totally congruent with your actions. To say "I believe in a healthy body" and to practice eating in unhealthy ways dissolves trust in yourself. Congruent thought, emotions and behavior are strong indicators of your self-trust. And keep in mind that when you trust in yourself, you are trusting in God at the same time.

When you are incongruent with your thoughts, you are showing a lack of trust in the divinity that is your essence. Be honest about any incongruency. Identify it and trust in your ability to transcend it, and the energy that you need for this transformation will be attracted to you. But if you hang onto the incongruency, thinking one thing but behaving in disingenuous ways, you will sabotage your ability to trust in yourself and in the infinite wisdom as well.

As you practice surrendering, acknowledge

your fundamental richness rather than bemoaning the imagined poverty of your being. When you practice spiritual trust you are surrendering your ego, and all of its hallucinatory beliefs, to a higher power. You are just letting go and knowing that divine guidance is always with you.

⏱ Begin a meditation practice of contemplating the supreme principle that is beyond the pettiness of this world. Yes, it is *in* this world, but it is not blemished by this world. The mind needs and craves serenity. Meditation is not merely making the mind think that it is meditating. Meditation is, literally, the embodiment of truth and trust. It is in the purification of the mind that liberation reveals itself.

The practice of meditation is a powerful tool in my life. As a writer, I sometimes write for hours and everything flows magically. Then a time comes when there are no more words. I want to write and nothing happens. No matter how hard I want to write, there is no writing taking place.

At these moments I have learned to leave the typewriter and to sit quietly, closing my eyes and surrendering. I don't know what I surrender to, but I simply let go and attempt to purify my mind. Then, after some time of simply surrendering meditatively, I seem to tap into something that is a source of inspiration, and I write page after page with no idea where it is coming from. This process of closing my eyes and becoming serene gives me the ability to tap into that source of inspiration. And the word "inspiration" comes from "in spirit."

This is trust. This is grace. It is knowing that I can literally confront myself in a spirit of serenity and that what I seek will be attracted to me. This is the energy of manifesting, and it comes most frequently when the mind is quiet. It is the quiet mind that comes in contact with the truth.

When we meditate, we come into contact with the part of us that is truth. The surrendering process helps us to use this truth in our daily pursuits. It is the same with trust. Surrender to it through your quiet moments of serenity and you will know the truth of this principle.

This second spiritual principle of manifesting leads us to a higher place within ourselves. It gives us the confidence to trust in something other than that which we perceive with our senses. It illuminates within us the knowing that there is far more to this journey than what we observe, and we come to trust in this knowing to a point where peace serves as a serene substitute for doubt and anxiety.

When you trust, you know. And a knowing cannot be silenced by the contrary opinions of anyone you encounter. You will be independent of the good opinion of others when this trust becomes your way of life. You will not need to prove yourself to anyone, or to convince anyone of the rightness of your views.

You will be a silent sage, moving through this material plane with a knowing that you have tapped into a source of inspiration that provides you with all the sustenance you need. Indeed, you will begin to see how this earth plane is really a very big part of you, more so than you might ever have imagined. And this is the subject matter for the third principle of manifesting.

YOU ARE NOT AN ORGANISM IN AN ENVIRONMENT: YOU ARE AN ENVIRONORGANISM

———————— ☺ ☺ ☺ *The Third Principle*

*O*ne of the reasons the idea of being able to manifest is so foreign to most of us is because we have been brought up to believe that as individuals we are separate from our environment. We think it is our role to dominate our environment and describe ourselves as individuals within the environment. Armed with this kind of logic, we are diminished in our ability to sense our connection to our environment.

Because of our sense of disconnection we believe we do not have the power to attract what we want from our environment. Consequently, we feel it is merely a matter of luck or happenstance when we succeed in manifesting. When we change this idea about ourselves, we activate our ability to manifest and see it as a function of our divinity rather than as being an impossibility or an incident of luck or coincidence.

This third principle of manifesting begins with the understanding that it is absolutely impossible to describe ourselves as separate from our environment. I am coining a new word, a neologism, for the purpose of articulating this principle. For the rest of this chapter consider yourself as an "environorganism." This word signifies that there is absolutely no difference between you and your environment. You are your environment, and even more significantly, for the purposes of this book, your environment is you.

OUR NATURE AS AN ENVIRONORGANISM

Try thinking of the external world, your environment, as your extended body. That is, you are not separate from the external world you see. In this concept it is impossible to describe yourself without including your surroundings. In fact, it is not even possible to see or hear yourself as a separate entity apart from your environment.

For example, describe yourself walking, just you walking. There cannot be walking without also describing whatever it is you are walking upon. Without the floor or the ground, there would only be your legs moving back and forth, and, of course, that is not walking. Your experience of walking also includes the air you are breathing while you are walking, the gravity that keeps you from floating off into space, the pebbles, or carpet, or sand, or cement that you walk on and the makeup of these elements in the pebbles and carpet, and on and on.

In addition to your walking as an example of you as an environorganism, examine the page that you are reading in this moment. What do you actually see? Black ink formed into words that you are reading. Try to imagine these words without the presence of the background upon which they are printed. The white page on which the words are printed does not receive your primary attention, yet this page you are holding as a unit of a book creates a meaning in combination with the individual units of print called words. The environment in which those words are inseparably enmeshed is the page itself.

In this analogy, you are the words and your background is everything upon which you are imprinted. This principle is important to understand if you are going to become a manifester. Just as the stars in the sky would be impossible to perceive without the background of the dark sky, and you couldn't see your own body or the body of anyone else without a background that is in contrast to that body, so does this principle apply to you.

You cannot be described independent of your environment, and I invite you to shift your awareness away from yourself as an organism in the environment to yourself as an extension of your environment and always inseparable from it. The result of this thinking will be that you begin to see that everything in your environment is a part of you and vice versa. Your environment is not something that you must either push or it will push you around. It is an extension of yourself, just as you are an extension of the environment.

This is a unique concept to grasp. It is imperative, however, for understanding the premise of this book. You are both distinct and inseparable from your environment.

BEING AN INDIVIDUAL AND AN ENVIRONMENT SIMULTANEOUSLY

Have you ever seen a person with a front but without a back? Have you ever seen a person with an outside but without an inside? These rhetorical questions are meant to stimulate you to consider how you can be differentiated and undifferentiated at the same time, and why this is important in learning to manifest your life as you choose.

The nature of this physical world is essentially that of waves. Each wave of energy that makes up a physical mass has a crest or a peak and a nadir or a valley. These tops and bottoms of the wave are always easy to identify as separate, yet they are always together. You cannot ever get a bucketful of peaks and observe them independent of their corresponding valleys. This is the fundamental feature of nature. The north and south poles of a magnet are always together, yet always distinct. Your front always has a back, your inside always has an outside, and now you must extend this understanding outward as well.

Of course you are an individual who functions within this environment, and it is possible to describe both you and your environment with separate identifying terminology that all of us would understand. But, you must also remember that you cannot separate you from your environment either. You are distinct, just as the tops of the waves are distinct from the bottoms, but you are irrevocably connected to the outer world just as that bottom of the wave always has a top.

When you begin to see this simple truth, mystical experiences of manifesting also open up to you as a genuine possibility. Most of us have failed to grasp this little truth, and it has led us on a disastrous course of feeling that because we are separate from our environment, we must exercise control over it. When we do this, we, of course, are showing not only a lack of respect for our environment, but for our own basic nature as an environorganism as well.

PUSHING NATURE AROUND OR SEEING IT AS OURSELVES

When we think of ourselves as distinct from our environment, we take on a posture of exercising control over it. This kind of thinking leads us into destructive behavior on both the collective and the personal levels.

We destroy forests, swamps, mountains, rivers, wildlife or anything else that obstructs profit and convenience or for something we call "advancing" civilization. We defend these activities without understanding that we are also destroying ourselves. Ultimately we will make earth uninhabitable if we fail to see that we are killing a part of ourselves with this wanton disregard for nature.

We all need to begin to experience ourselves as part of our total environment. Then perhaps we will discontinue trying to beat that same environment into submission. We fail to treat it with love, gentleness and respect because we are convinced that it is something other than ourselves that we are defeating. As we have seen, we cannot be described independent of our environment any more than our outside can be described without our inside.

The idea of ourselves as an environorganism commands our respect for everything that we encounter. When we can respect that which appears to be external to us, we will build to live in harmony with, rather than in control over, our environment.

In our personal lives, recognizing nature as ourselves opens up an entire new world of manifestation. We see ourselves in an intelligent world. Thus, the intelligence that is in myself is also in my environment. With this awareness we tend to see the connection to everything much more clearly. We know that whatever appears to be lacking in our lives is really due to our having been misinformed when we were taught that what seems to be missing can be found outside us.

As an environorganism, I know that the energy of what appears to be missing in my personal environment and the energy of my own body (inside and outside, front and back) is all the same. So, anything I view as lacking is because I see myself as removed from what I want rather than as connected to it.

This is the beginning of the awareness that you can attract everything to yourself because you are already inextricably attached to it at an energy level. The notion of viewing it as unavailable begins to disappear and you see manifesting as nothing more than materializing an aspect of yourself of which you have previously been unaware.

You will see yourself not only in your environment, but in everything and everyone that is a part of that environment. Your new faith will no longer permit you to see anything as separate. The separateness will always be there, just as the peak of the wave is separate from the trough, but they will remain inseparable even though separate, different yet undifferentiated at the same time. You will have fused the dichotomy that prevents you from putting this connective energy to work. You will begin to view yourself as an organic part of this world rather than as a separate entity in this world.

SEEING YOURSELF AS AN ORGANIC PART OF THIS WORLD

There is a popular belief that we "come into this world." Thus we are continuously embracing the idea that who we are and where we come from are two different worlds. The essence of this third spiritual principle for manifesting your destiny is that there is no separation, and rather than coming into this world as a construction project, that you actually grow out of it.

Take a look at a plum tree and examine how plums appear in our world. You plant a seed and the tree grows, ultimately blossoming and producing plums. The intelligence that is in the plum is in this world, and so, too, is it in the seed, the blossom, the trunk, the branches and the roots. Every single element of the plum tree has plum intelligence built into it. We do not say that plums show up from the spiritual world of plum essence, and then become physical earth-plane fruit. In fact, as we look at a plum tree, we could say with all candor that it plums. Every year the thing just plums.

In the same way that a plum tree plums, you, too, grow out of this world, with the same energy that is in every aspect of your being. Were you to look at the earth from a distance you would observe that it has rocks, oceans, vegetation, and that the thing actually peoples. You are a result of what the universe is doing on a conscious level, just as a wave is what the ocean is doing and a plum is what the plum tree is doing. The intelligence that is you, unseen as it may be, is you in every stage of your creation and life experience, and it is also the same in every other person as well as in all things in our physical world.

Most of us were taught quite the contrary. Creation is generally thought of as divided into the spiritual realm of the unseen and the physical world of matter. Also, that we are the result of an act of construction, and rather than growing out of the world, we were put into it. This, of course, reinforces the idea of powerlessness in having anything to do with the act of creation. To empower yourself to become a co-creator in the affairs of your life, you will have to leave these old ideas behind, but mind you, they do not die easily. The conditioning process is embedded in the bedrock of your existence.

When you come to see yourself as growing out of this world, you see that the native intelligence that was in the very seed of your procreation is an energy flowing through everything in your world. You and the environment of that growth process are distinctly identifiable but always connected. Inseparable in the same way as your breathing and the air you breathe, your walking and the ground upon which you walk and your thoughts and the organism with which you think.

Notice that everyone breathes the same air, walks on the same ground and thinks as an organism, just like you. You are, indeed, connected to all of these beings. It is not an accident that someone living in a distant country, with different outward physical characteristics and a separate language, could die and donate his or her liver or kidney or cornea to you, and it would accommodate the life force flowing in you. This idea of growing out of the world or being a result of the earth peopling as a plum tree plums is advantageous to the process of manifesting your own destiny. It empowers you with the wisdom of creation rather than making you a puppet whose strings are controlled by external forces.

When we believe that what is outside me is not me, and that we are not a part of the peopling process of the earth, we cultivate an attitude of estrangement and hostility. This mentality leads us to talk of our conquest of the environment, which means that we cannot capitalize on the awareness of being a connected being. The need to conquer puts us at odds with the world.

A profoundly important Native American saying is: "No tree has branches so foolish as to fight among themselves." Imagine the result of such behavior by the tree! The tree and all of its parts would die from such an absurdity. Yet that is precisely what we do when we see ourselves as divided from all of the other people who are being peopled from the same divine intelligence.

We grow out of our world and are the result of what the divine intelligence is doing, and we can never lose that connection. You might think of yourself as a symptom of the universe rather than as a stranger in this universe.

What we have all come to think of as the spirit within us is actually that divine, unseen intelligence that caused you, and continues to cause you to grow out of this world. It, too, is inseparable from your physical essence, your environment and everyone and everything else in this universe. If you think otherwise, then you reinforce your inability to influence your destiny and to manifest or attract anything to you.

When you know that you grow out of this world just as an apple does from an apple tree, then you identify with this spiritual essence. It is in identification with this inner essence that you make your connection to everything else. And it is with this connection that you begin to attract your desires to your physical world. This power of attraction will be the subject matter of the fourth principle described in this book.

For now, I want you to gain a clear sense of how you are actually growing out of the world. I want you to perceive the difference in this concept from one that promulgates our arrival here from a separate world by a power that is outside us. You are not a momentary flash of embodied consciousness between two eternal blacknesses. You are an essence that is eternally growing in this world, a world in which the spirit and the manifestation of that spirit appear to be different to the senses, and indeed they are, but they are also connected. You are both of these essences at once.

It is this awareness that is crucial as you proceed along this manifesting path. It is a power, but make no mistake about it, contrary to what your ego might tell you, you do not get to own this power exclusively.

THE POWER IS IN YOU BUT IS NOT YOURS ALONE

The power and the magic of this world cannot be reserved for the exclusive use of anyone, including you. It is available at all times; however, it does not belong to anyone. What you are doing as an environ-organism is making contact with an energy that is beyond the dualism of the earth plane, and yet is connected to it at the same time, separate but distinct.

The way to make this contact is to understand this energy. Everything on the physical plane experiences lightness and darkness. If it were always light we would not have a concept of dark. But there is something that could never know darkness. That is the source of all light, the sun. The source is beyond the duality of the physical plane. It is this source of energy that you want to contact when you are empowering yourself.

You do not own the energy of the sun, but it is always available to you. That energy is not subject to the laws of duality, nor is your spirit, which is the source of your divine power. But it is still you, and yours to use.

You cannot own this power any more than you can own and control the environment. To own it means you separate from it. There becomes an owner and that which is owned, and this violates the principle of you as an environorganism. You are a holistic being with both nondualistic energy and the energy of the physical plane as a part of your being at your disposal.

You are a whole being. You therefore need a holistic view of yourself as an environorganism in order to understand yourself. To conceptualize yourself as a spiritual and physical being separate from your environment is to remove any potential for knowing your holistic state. As a holistic being you shatter the illusion of your separateness and reveal your connection to everything. This empowers you in a way that the ego-driven self could never contemplate.

SEEING YOURSELF AS A HOLOGRAM

One of the most intriguing ways to see yourself in the way that I am describing in this third principle is to look at a hologram and then project yourself into this viewpoint. If, somehow, you were able to see all of humanity along with everything else that exists simultaneously, you would have a vision of the hologrammatic nature of the universe. As it is, you are stuck being able to see only tiny segments of the earth at one time.

A hologram is a three-dimensional photographic image obtained with laser beams. The unique thing about a hologram is that one small segment contains the entire picture. When one tiny piece of the hologram is broken off and projected, it shows an image of the entire object.

The hologram is a perfect representation for you as an environorganism. Your environment includes everyone, alive and dead, and you can draw their energy to you because, from a hologrammatic viewpoint, they are you. You are one little physical image that reflects all of humanity when projected spiritually upon the cosmic screen. Each and every one of us is the whole of humanity. You cannot escape this conclusion.

The understanding of holograms can be applied intrinsically and extrinsically. One tiny segment of your body can be cut off and projected through a laser beam, and your entire body will be reflected from that one tiny piece. Each and every cell of your being contains the energy of your entire being. On an extrinsic level, you are one of those segments that reflect all of humanity as a hologram.

Unfortunately, the peoples of the world have yet to apply this hologrammatic understanding to their living. Seeing ourselves as connected to all of humanity is an idea whose time will come, and it will not be stopped. History shows us how we have carved ourselves up into nations with various ideologies such as capitalism, socialism, totalitarianism, communism, monarchism and democracy that often transcend the importance of humanity itself. We have classified ourselves on the basis of physical appearance and nationalistic identifications such as Italian, American and Japanese. We have further subdivided ourselves into classes based upon our economic levels or the colors of our collars.

Countries are further divided between the political right and left and religious beliefs, and the division continues right on down into families and, eventually, into individuals. The process of division is the opposite of the hologram model of our reality.

Essentially, like it or not, human beings are the same everywhere. We share the emotions of fear, love, hate and jealousy. We also share our life-giving blood, intermingling it for the survival of those who need it, and we have the same internal organs and thoughts. Yet our egos persist in the work of division.

When we look at our individual selves there is also the inclination to divide ourselves, which leads us away from our divine nature and removes us from the world of manifesting our destiny. We need to monitor the internal conflict with which we divide ourselves. The ego creates divisive thoughts such as the following: the difference between what I am and what I should be; how I behave and how I should behave; how I used to be and how I am today; what I have been told by others is what I should be; how messed up I am in reality; what I think and how I feel; how I look and how much better others look; how much I make, how much others make and how much I need. The list is potentially endless.

All of this conflict as a result of our propensity to divide and subdivide ourselves at the world, national, social or individual level is an expression of chaos. We cannot bring order to the world or to our lives as long as we fail to recognize that, in reality, all human beings are holograms of humanity. We all reflect the whole, and it is essential for us to begin to think in this way.

When you perceive yourself in the hologram that is humanity, you connect on an energy level to everyone else in your environment. An environorganism most truly is a reflection of it all, and this energy that you share is shared by all. This awareness gives you the option to tap into this universal energy anywhere, at any time, by metaphorically projecting yourself to reflect the whole. When you can do this projecting without doubt or reservation, you can literally see how your inner thoughts and desires are not only within you, but are within the whole of humanity, which is abundantly boundless. This is accomplished by simply changing your beliefs from a separate ego to that of an environorganism.

As an environorganism, you are a single individual who is only a part of the picture at the same time that you contain the whole panorama. Moreover, the content of your consciousness, which differs from person to person, is also hologrammatic in nature. Consciousness is the mental condition of being aware. Your individual thoughts, while they form only a part of the total picture of human consciousness, simultaneously contain the whole of human consciousness.

Like a hologram, your thoughts reflect the thoughts of all. The power of your thoughts in this hologrammatic view can be projected in such a way as to connect to all of humanity. Your thoughts are, literally, connected to the thoughts of everyone else, as are your emotions, your desires, your total inner world. You can learn to use this connection to nurture your own divinity and, therefore, by definition, the divinity of all of humanity.

The nature of a hologram and the nature of you as an environorganism are one and the same. The energy that comprises your humanity is in everything around you. You are it, it is you. You are not separate from it. The Bhagavad Gita summarizes this point of view as profoundly as I've ever found. Commit these holy words to memory as you practice the art of spiritual manifesting in your daily life. They will serve you well wherever you are, and in whatever way you believe your current life circumstances are incomplete.

He who sees that the Lord of all is ever the same in all that is—immortal in the field of mortality—he sees the truth. And when a man sees that the God in himself is the same God in all that is, he hurts not himself by hurting others. Then he goes, indeed, to the highest path.

The key phrase in this profound passage is "in all that is." This includes you and me and everything that is. It is you. You are not separate from it. Use some of the following suggestions to implement this understanding and truly experience this third principle of spiritual manifesting.

SUGGESTIONS FOR LIVING THIS PRINCIPLE

⊙ Make a conscious effort to check yourself when you begin to think in ways that reflect separateness. Imagine yourself as a part of all that you see and make an internal attempt to project the energy of your thoughts into all that is alive on the planet.

Substitute the pronoun "us" for the pronoun "them," and send sacred energy to co-workers, family, strangers and people that you only see in faraway places on television. Silently say, "I am these people," "I am also in those trees and clouds," "We truly are the world and I am not separate from anyone or anything." This inner practice will help you to embrace the concept of you as an environorganism rather than an organism in an environment.

⊙ Contemplate the energy that is your life force. Forget about your body and your thoughts, and focus attention on the invisible life force that sustains your very being, which is also known as *chi* or *prana*. See if you can sense it objectively and also try to do the same thing with the energy of someone close to you. Watch that person and forget about his or her body. Center your attention on the idea that you share the same energy, and so you are the same person at that energy level.

Becoming an observer of your energy and the energy of those around you is a way of putting you into contact with the spiritual essence of everyone and everything. Awareness of this connection will help you begin to use this energy to attract the objects of your desire, since this life force is also present in all that you wish to manifest into your life.

⊙ Trust in the wisdom of your feelings. If you feel it, it is true for you. You can avoid being controlled by attitudes that belong to others by not placing your trust in something your heart does not feel.

This is accomplished by trusting the wisdom of your inner feelings, which flow from trust of your experience of life. When you trust your feelings, you trust the energy that is the life force of the universe. Those feelings you know to be true are the contact with that life force and should never be ignored in favor of a belief that your heart wisdom contradicts.

⊙ Practice being gentle, respectful and loving toward the life force in all things. In other words, behave as if the God in all life really mattered.

I live near the ocean for most of the year, either

in Florida or Hawaii. I was walking along the beach in Florida one morning when thousands of small, silver fish washed up on the shore. They were all jumping around and gasping for water. I began throwing the fish back into the ocean, which was now a bit calmer after the waves that had beached the silver fish.

As I was throwing the fish back into the water, a man walked by and laughed at my efforts. He said something like, "Can't you see how hopeless your task is? There are thousands of fish on the shoreline, and your efforts are not making any difference at all." I bent back down and threw in another fish and responded, "It made a difference to that one." Remind yourself that your efforts do make a difference, even if you think they are minuscule compared to the magnitude of the problem.

Being gentle, respectful and loving to one other person or creature has major significance for you and the other. The energy of love is sent out into the universe and connects with the same loving essence that is in all things. This does not deny a natural food chain, but extends love, thanks, respect and gentleness to all, even when it is a part of your diet.

The energy of that food is also life sustaining, and eventually, every creature and every being becomes food for other beings, including yourself. In essence, we are all tomorrow's food. The universe gobbles up all form and turns it into new form, while the energy that is warehoused in that form is eternal.

☉ Determine that you will spend some time each day alone and in silence, meditating on this principle. Repeat the principle over and over as a silent mantra: "I am not an organism in an environment, I am an environorganism." By repeating these words to yourself you will eventually begin to project this reality outward.

This is the beginning of your manifestation project, because manifesting is nothing more than materializing a new aspect of yourself to which you have always been connected on a spiritual level.

☉ Make the spaces of your life as sacred as possible. In your living space bless all that surrounds you, and fill your space with the life that plants, flowers and animals bring. Spend some time contemplating your living space as a holy place.

The more you bring your environment alive with sacred thoughts and feelings, the more you will feel spiritually connected. An attitude of sacred space automatically attracts more to your world than an attitude of indifference or hostility. A hostile environment breeds discontent and keeps what you need and desire from manifesting in your life.

This is uncomfortably obvious in large cities, where very little respect has been paid to the immediate environs, where trees have been cut down, parks removed, and most of it replaced with concrete, stores, high-rises and freeways. The soul is removed when the space is not honored by builders or residents.

What manifests is a hostile, frightening, non-loving world with people to match. Restoring nature and all that is natural to your life and to the places where it has been forfeited in the name of growth and profits in our larger social living areas is one way of bringing back the energy that will manifest love, happiness and prosperity.

The Sufi poet Rumi wrote a poem, almost a millennium ago, called "The Seed Market" that reflects this consciousness.

The Seed Market

Can you find another market like this?
Where,
with your one rose
you can buy hundreds of rose gardens?

Where,
for one seed
you get a whole wilderness?

For one weak breath,
the divine wind?

You've been fearful
Of being absorbed in the ground,
or drawn up by the air.

Now, your waterbead lets go
and drops into the ocean,
where it came from.

It no longer has the form it had,
but it's still water.
The essence is the same.

This giving up is not a repenting.
It's a deep honoring of yourself.

When the ocean comes to you as a lover,
marry, at once, quickly,
for God's sake!

Don't postpone it!
Existence has no better gift.

No amount of searching
will find this.

A perfect falcon, for no reason,
has landed on your shoulder,
and become yours.

—FROM *The Essential Rumi*
TRANSLATIONS BY COLEMAN BARKS
WITH JOAN MOYNE

☉ Become aware of how your judgments prevent you from connecting to whatever you are judging. A judgment is a definition of yourself as separate from that which you are judging. Remember that it is possible to look out on the world and not condemn it, to have absolutely no judgment or interpretation of it but to just allow it to be.

The ego is the part that keeps you attached to an idea of separation which, of course, inhibits your awareness of this third principle. Your ego analyzes, condemns, defines, evaluates, interprets and judges almost everything. Work hard each day at just letting go and seeing yourself as a part of all of those people and things that you are judging. When the judgment disappears, it does so because you have realized that you are really a part of that which you are judging. Your judgment is only a definition of yourself.

As an environorganism you will find judgment almost impossible and this will free you to use that energy in a far more productive and loving way. That is, to manifest what you desire rather than to judge others.

☉ Have fun with the idea of yourself as a hologram. If you remember that you are a tiny piece of humanity, reflected in your own little image and personality, then you have a green light to reflect the humanity that you would like in your world. You are one tiny bit of a six-billion-or-so-piece hologram, and you reflect all of those six billion pieces at every given moment of your life.

This is a difficult concept for your rational brain to grasp but, on the other hand, take a look at a three-dimensional hologram sometime and try to figure out with your rational mind how one little sliver can reflect the whole. This is not a knowing for your left brain. It is for your heart. View yourself in this way, from your heart, and you will create a scintillating experience of how powerful you really are in this big hologram of a world.

This is the third principle of spiritual manifestation. We are all simultaneously our own beings and all that is outside us as well. We cannot ever separate ourselves from our environment while we are in a physical body. Knowing this puts us in touch with the energy of attraction that is the subject matter of the fourth principle.

YOU CAN ATTRACT TO YOURSELF
WHAT YOU DESIRE

———————— ☺ ☺ ☺ *The Fourth Principle*

*T*he central notion of manifesting is the understanding that you have within yourself the ability to
attract the objects of your desire. This idea may still
seem to you to be out of your power. But, if you have
understood the previous three principles, then you are
beginning to know that this power is within you. Being
able to attract your desires may seem more likely when
you consider how things are created from the spirit
world of the formless seemingly moving into the material world.

In one of the most intriguing sentences in the New
Testament, St. Paul addresses this process of creation.
He said it this way: "Things which are seen are not
made of things which do appear." St. Paul is telling us

that the creative energy is neither solid nor restricted. The physical world of form originates in something other than form itself, even though we know it is all *one* world, when viewed from a hologrammatic perspective.

St. Paul's words form the basis for my writing about this principle and for several of those to come in this book. I believe they suggest how energy informs our ability to attract what we desire. St. Paul is giving us a clue about manifesting our desires into the world of matter.

ENERGY AS A FORCE WE CAN TAP

In a film about his boyhood, Albert Einstein describes picking up a compass and watching in fascination as the needle moved when he changed direction. He said that he became obsessed with understanding the invisible force that moved the compass needle. Where was the force located? Who controlled it? Why did it always work? What was it made of? Were there places where it didn't operate? These are the natural questions of an inquiring genius.

This force has many characteristics that are quite impossible to detect with our physical senses. We call the force energy. Energy is in all things in our universe and has an impact upon objects around it with something that we describe as the power of attraction. In magnetic fields we can easily see it at work, yet we are unable to detect the formless energy with our sensory apparatus. The force is there, attracting and repelling, and it is everywhere on our planet.

If it is everywhere, then it is also within us. It seems unlikely that our senses will inform us any better than they help us comprehend how a magnetic pole works. We can see the results, but the force itself is always elusive and in motion.

Our planet is in a perpetual state of spinning, orbiting and hurtling through space. Everything on the planet is a part of this movement, even though it appears to our senses that we are motionless. You are on the planet. The energy that moves it moves you. The energy that is in the very essence of the planet is in you. It is magnetic and electrical in nature, with the force of attraction built into it.

The essence of the fourth principle of manifestation is that we can utilize this energy because we are this energy. We can use this universal energy to bring to us objects of our desire, because the same energy that is in what we desire is also in us and vice versa. It becomes a matter of alignment and will that allows us to tap into this force.

Bringing things into the physical world is a process that we call creation. What we create involves the use of the same power in all that is created. It is only a matter of degree. There is absolutely no difference in the power that brings anything from the world of waves into the world of particles, and the power that brings your thoughts or mental pictures into form. I encourage you to reread that previous sentence and commit it to memory.

The world of spirit from which all matter derives and the world of matter literally comprise one harmonious whole. They are separate but always together, just like the peak of the wave and its base, separate but forming an inseparable whole. To put this into perspective, think of manifesting as nothing more than transforming waves of possibilities into particles of reality. The transforming process requires energy. This energy is invisible but is always in everything, including us.

Your thoughts and visualizations are your source of manifesting. It is this energy that you want to activate and make work for you. The mental-picturing process and its application to the manifesting process are something that you can experience when you are in a state of complete faith. There is a part of you that knows you can attract what you desire with this energy.

YOUR MENTAL PICTURES AND THE POWER OF ATTRACTION

There is a power within you that allows you to form a thought or picture. This mental-picturing power is the energy of attraction that is in all creative processes. Moreover, it is identical with the power of attraction. This power is the very substance of life.

You can't see, touch or hear this power, but it is within you. In using this power you are not in any way attempting to change or interfere with the laws of nature. You are fulfilling the laws. This undifferentiated power is the basis for the mysterious attraction that draws your desires to you.

It may help to think of yourself as a way that God has of particularizing. Then see your ability to formulate mental pictures as the divine creative power energizing through you. Can you see that the same creative energy that particularizes as yourself is what you use to manifest your desires? This power thrives on happiness, love, joy, contentment and peace. The more blissful and loving you are, the more the divine spirit particularizes within you and the more Godlike you become.

It is through your thoughts (or how you use your power to create a thought) that all creative energy is attracted to you. If your mental pictures are of being surrounded by things and conditions that you desire, and they are rooted in joy and faith, your creative thoughts will attract these surroundings and conditions into your life. This may sound a bit too much like wishful thinking, but, trust me, it is far more than wishing or hoping.

What is different is that you recognize that the power to even have a thought is a divine power, and then with this recognition of its sacredness you form a vision or a mental picture. Finally, you hold it lovingly in place with the inner knowledge that the God force that brought everything in the universe into existence also created you. The form that this energy will take will be controlled and directed by your will or your mental picturing. It is waiting to take any direction that you decide.

It is important to be able to think in terms that are beyond our senses. Energy is the creative life force that allows us to do the things that we observe with our senses. It is an invisible force that supports the substance of our material life. This energy gives us the power to have thoughts, and it is the same as the energy of everything that appears to be external to us.

Your mental pictures are integral to this power of attraction, and to the subsequent authentic experience of creative energy when you are able to put these images into practice.

THE PRACTICE OF MENTAL PICTURING

The most important thing to remember as you practice mental picturing for the purposes of manifesting your desires is that humans never create anything. Our function is not to create, but to attract, combine and distribute what already exists.

Creations are really new combinations of already existing materials.

I am not speaking here of creating energy, but of transforming one form of energy into another. Our creative power is the ability to convert the energy of our thoughts into a newly materialized form. Manifestation is the result.

There is one indispensable condition for the manifestation of that picture into the visible and concrete world. The world of spirit is immune to the concept of time and space. Therefore, the picture must either be formed here and now or not at all. Once you have this awareness you will understand the necessity of picturing the fulfillment of your desire as if it is already accomplished on the spiritual plane.

That's right, you must know within yourself that on

the invisible level of your being, what you desire is already in place. You must know that the energy is here and let the how take care of itself. That is, if the end is secured, the means is also handled and you let go, knowing that success is guaranteed.

This is not a prescription for idleness, but for letting go of worry, anxiety and fear. You will work on the formulation of your mental pictures, and you will do it knowing that the end has been secured. The intelligence of the spirit or the great impersonal power is acknowledged. You, too, are intelligence. What you are doing is allowing one intelligence to cooperate with the other. It will not do it for you, it will do it with you.

You impress upon the universal mind the object of your desire, and you calmly and knowingly proceed to act upon that picture, allowing the greater intelligence, and your own, which is a part of that greater intelligence, to work through you to produce the results. You abandon all fear and return to the affairs of your life assured that the necessary conditions will soon come into view or are already there. Stay alert for any small circumstance that indicates the first sprouting of the seed that you have planted in the universal mind, and allow it to form in your life as a growing materialization.

I admit that this is not something that is consistent with our conditioning. But in order to make ourselves manifesters, we have to shed old beliefs and adopt an inner wisdom that helps us to stop manifesting the circumstances we want to change.

The more you do this mental picturing with faith and enthusiasm, the more likely you are to see it manifesting. What you are doing is literally visualizing in detail what it is that you want to manifest. You detach from the outcome and how it will be accomplished. You are not in the business of creating, but of attracting to yourself what is already in creation, and allowing the energy of the spirit to transform into the energy of matter. You see in great detail what it is that you want, and you repeatedly affirm this picture with faith in the absolute power that is in all things, including yourself.

You can picture yourself healthy, your business thriving, your sales quotas being met, your relationships healing, your house selling, finances coming your way or anything you desire. The key is to repeat these mental pictures until the truth of what you are affirming resonates within you without an ounce of doubt.

I find the best times for doing this deep work are early in the morning and just before I retire for the night. I also find the use of specific sounds and affirmations very useful. They are described in the seventh and eighth principles.

I am certain that a key question in your mind at this point is, "Yes, but what if it doesn't materialize as I picture it?" This is worthy of your attention.

WHEN IT APPEARS THAT IT ISN'T WORKING

It is the way of the ego to try to force things when they are not going our way. We all know the folly of getting down on our knees and tugging away at the new vegetable shoots as they start to appear in the spring.

They need to grow at their own pace, and they will flourish at precisely the right time.

If your picture does not manifest in the time span that you have designated, relax and retreat to your knowing that it is already in place in the spiritual realm. The energy is there by virtue of the power of your visualizing. Time is simply not a recognizable feature of the all-creating wisdom. Another facet that explains why your pictures are not showing up in the material world is the frequency with which you may be changing your pictures. The power you are working with is a sensitive force requiring dedicated and consistent mental picturing.

You may also be attempting to misuse your power by placing restrictions and contingencies on the universal intelligence. This all-creating wisdom, the originating principle, is not in any way dependent on specific people or things. It has no past, and it knows no future. It is in the eternal now, and most important for you to know, it creates its own vehicles through which it operates. If you begin ordering it around and making demands or insisting that it work through a specific channel, it will not accede to your requirements.

You will find it impossible to manifest if you are visualizing without an authentic will that is sufficiently steady to overcome any contrary idea or lack of faith in your own divine connection to God. The second principle in this book was about faith and trust. Reread that if you feel it needs to be reinforced. Your trust in the power of attraction is absolutely necessary. All of this is most effectively done in a private manner.

THE VALUE OF SECRECY

Making conscious contact with the highest all-creating infinite power is a very private matter. The *naguals* (a Native American term for spiritual masters or sorcerers) and mystics who practice and teach these methods guard their privacy. Moreover, they consider it a violation of their sacred trust to talk to others about their abilities and the "coincidences" of good fortune.

When we speak to others about our efforts to manifest, our power is weakened. In general, when we describe these activities it is because the ego has entered the picture. This kind of approach considerably dissipates our power of attraction.

It is human nature to talk to others about problems because we want to alleviate their influence in our life. By sharing, we hope to relieve some of the pressure of the problem. So, too, when we articulate our power to attract something, our attention shifts to the reactions of those in whom we are confiding. Energy is dispersed in the direction of their reactions in the same way that it is when we share problems. The moment a thought is presented to another it is weakened. Maintain privacy concerning your own unique, possibly mysterious to others, powers to attract to you what you desire.

Your etheric energy body is yours and yours alone. You can learn to project your energy outward and have an impact on the external world in ways that you have perhaps never even considered before. However, in order to tap into this extraordinary energy and use it in the co-creation process, it must remain yours and yours alone. The moment you discuss it with anyone who is alive today is the moment it diminishes. Your energy shifts to an interest in the good opinion of the other.

This higher energy, which is infinite, must create its own vehicles for manifesting, and it does so in the privacy of those vehicles. This highest infinite, all-knowing wisdom is a life force that you will recognize when you become familiar with its nature.

THE NATURE OF THE VITAL FORCE

It is difficult to comprehend a force that we cannot see, touch, hear or smell and still know that it exists. It is similar to electricity. You plug in your appliance and you cannot see, touch, smell or hear anything happening, but your electric hair dryer responds when you press the On switch.

The life force is electrical in nature, regardless of where it appears to be localized. In our own bodies, the *chi,* or *prana,* the life force, flows in tiny charges along our nerves from cell to cell. Ancient Hawaiian healers known as kahunas believed that thought forms could be carried back and forth on this current. They believed that thoughts had shadowy, microscopic and almost invisible bodies. This kind of knowing permitted the kahunas to participate in phenomenal healing practices. They were able to transmit the will to heal along these currents and to facilitate health where disease had existed.

I have visualized a current flowing between my

thought and a painful or ill area of my body. Using my will and visualizing the current, I sent messages from my will to those areas to be free of the pain, or to heal the wound. I have had stunning results. The shadowy bodies of my thoughts became things I could send along this invisible current, and because I knew it would work, it did.

This is a good way to think of the vital force that is the all-creating God force as well. It is invisible, electrical in nature, always flowing and always attracted to that which plugs into its source. A second characteristic of the life force energy is that it is always expanding, and it is unlimited in supply.

The nature of the universe is abundance. It goes on beyond our concepts of beginnings and endings and boundaries. When we think we have it categorized and locked into a time-space boundary, it expands beyond our awareness almost as if it must move farther away from observation. This force is always moving, ever expanding and unlimited.

You are an aspect of that force, and therefore you, too, are flowing, ever expanding and unlimited. If you study yourself under a microscope with high magnification you will see that you are empty spaces with ever moving particles that have no material form. When you turn up the magnification on the particles, you see that they are moving at incredible speeds, beyond your capacity to measure them. When you look outward through the telescope, you see the same phenomena. That is, the universe within you and outside of you work in the same fashion.

It is your nature to be able to attract, to expand, to be unlimited. The force is in you, and the force is outside you. The force *is* you. By knowing the nature of this force and seeing yourself as a divine expression of it, and by going within to the power that permits you to picture a desire, and then tapping that power with a private, loving, cheerful knowing, you are on your way to using this vital force in ways that were unavailable to you with your conditioned view of yourself.

Here are a few suggestions for putting these ideas into practice in your life as you begin mastering this fourth spiritual principle of manifestation.

SOME IDEAS FOR PUTTING THIS PRINCIPLE TO WORK

⊙ When first arising in the morning, take a few moments to be alone and ask yourself, "How did the conditions of my life that I would like to change first come about?" "How can I facilitate making conscious contact with my unlimited, invisible source of energy?"

These two questions, when repeatedly considered, will begin to create their own answers. Remind yourself that it is spirit that gives life and movement to anything and everything, including you. It is that which causes your very existence. Therefore, you are truly asking to join into the spirit of your life.

You will soon realize that the conditions of

your life have been manifested by you, even though you were not conscious of bringing them about. Your thoughts and mental pictures of lack, scarcity, self-absorption, authoritarianism, illness, guilt, worry and the like have been put into the universal spirit and have manifested in your life. The second question will flow from your answer to the first.

You can hasten your conscious contact by radiating a totally new kind of mental picture while applying this fourth principle.

☉ Explore the possibility that the reason you believe that life is limiting is because you have assumed limitation to be in your life.

In the world of nature, life, love and beauty are visibly reproduced. You, too, are a part of nature. Does your view of life include the natural creative process reproducing within yourself? Or have you assumed an engineering view of life with a mechanical cause-and-effect conclusion?

Perhaps you can shift this awareness to seeing cause and effect as *a* law, but not *the* law. The law of originating mind is beyond the world of boundaries and measurement. You originated out of this law, and your imagination is a perfect example of this. No rule, no boundary, no form. Unlimited!

The source of your imagination is the divine source. It is here that you are now making contact with the eternally moving, always alive source of

light. Stay in this place within and you will know
conscious contact with the divine all-creating intelligence.

☉ Whatever picture you are able to create mentally
will assist you in knowing that the creative energy
is flowing through you. Your picture also provides
a direction for the flow of energy. And your picture gives substance to its eventual appearance in
material form.

You are not forcing anything with your picture. Strenuous effort is counterproductive to
manifesting because it sets up the idea of a force
that must be overcome. Get rid of the idea of
forcing anything or making demands. Instead,
imagine the creative knowing that allowed you to
come into this world of form. It is a loving, flowing, gentle, peaceful energy that is the source of
creation. Any effort to change that with demands
or strenuous effort will inhibit that flow.

☉ It is vital that you incorporate the concept of a
beginning and ending, or first and last with your
mental picturing. When you apply this alpha and
omega thinking you substantiate that first is the
thought, the beginning, which creates the form,
the end.

Thought finds form in something in time and
space. The expression of thought in the form is a
matter of gradual development, with a beginning
and an ending.

⊙ Never limit the spirit in any way. If you experience any kind of friction, know that it is an error in your thinking and picturing rather than proof that the creative force is working incorrectly. You cannot originate the originating force, you can only distribute it.

Just continue to tell the spirit what you want without telling it how you want it to happen. Then retreat, in faith and trust. You need not specify the details, only be ready to see it particularize in an endless array of possibilities. Stay alert for clues!

⊙ Keep your mental picturing to yourself. What you want to attract is a private matter between you and God. Discussing it with others will dissipate the energy in the direction of ego and the opinions of others.

Outwardly, be mysterious and silent while inwardly you have faith in your ability to make conscious contact with the energy that is the source of existence. Let go of the need to convince anyone of the rightness of your position. Remain independent of the good opinion of others and keep yourself fixed on your ability to attract whatever it is that you previously thought was missing in your life.

⊙ Examine all the supposed lacks and scarcities in your life. Then say to yourself, "I created all of this with my thoughts, conditioning, beliefs and actions." It is only by recognizing that you have always been attracting to yourself what you have been radiating out in the form of invisible energy that you will be able to use this same energy in a more productive manner.

Banish any guilt about your past actions. There is no past in the all-creative force of energy. There is only the universal now. Now you recognize that you have manifested all that you knew how to attract to yourself in the past. Now you are going to shift this awareness to a new way of being. You have attracted to yourself precisely what you have needed in all the days of your life that make up this universal now. In this same now, you are shifting to a new energy pattern that embraces this fourth principle of manifesting.

Nothing is outside you. You can attract anything when you know it already exists in the consciousness of your mind and has to materialize from your new thoughts. Be responsible and trusting and you will see your power of attraction working almost immediately.

☉ Thought is creative action. It is neither good nor bad. However, the thoughts that you dwell on determine what you will possess or not possess. What you think about is what you will become.

Be conscious of any thought or picture that will end up manifesting something that you do not want. If your conditioned way of thinking is in terms of pessimism, or impossibilities, or using your past misfortunes as reasons for not having a happier, more abundant life, decide to eradicate those thoughts. If you find yourself complaining to others, remind yourself that your complaints are a manifestation of your inner thoughts.

Make contact with the power that first allows you to have a thought and ask it to help and guide you to new ways of picturing. Once you start catching yourself in the middle of thoughts or complaints, you can initiate new pictures. This new picturing process is easy when you realize that you are connected to the power that allows you to attract to yourself what you desire.

As difficult as it is to fathom, because of ego-based conditioning, you are indeed one of the ways in which God has particularized in this material world.

⊙ Begin to act as if what you would like to attract is already in your life. If you want to create healing, formulate the picture, radiate out that energy to connect with the all-creating energy, be cheerful and trusting in your knowing, share it with no one and then begin acting in a new, healthy manner.

The universe will give you minimal clues to begin your new actions. Proceeding to act in the manner of your inner picture will hasten the process.

If you want to materialize more prosperity, then start the process of thinking abundantly and acting that way also. Give thanks for all that has manifested in your life. Examine ways in which to be grateful and take some risks, knowing that what you want to attract is already an energy that you share. Buy yourself something special and donate something to someone less fortunate, even if your ego balks!

⊙ Walt Whitman's *Leaves of Grass* is a special favorite of mine. I recommend that you browse through it daily as I do frequently. Here is a portion that speaks of our oneness with the divine energy.

Athwart the shapeless vastnesses of space.
How should I think, how breathe a single
    breath, how speak, if, out of myself,
I could not launch, to those, superior universes?

Swiftly I shrivel at the thought of God,
At nature and its wonders, Time and Space and
    Death,
But that I, turning, call to thee O soul, thou
    actual Me,
Thou matest Time, smilest content at Death,
And fillest, swellest full the vastness of Space.

The key phrase in this passage, for me, is ". . . thou actual Me. . . ." And so it is with you, no different than Walt Whitman or anyone else in the universe.

⊙   ⊙   ⊙

This concludes the fourth principle of spiritual manifestation. A summary of this principle tells us that there is an intelligence and a power in all of nature that is creative and responsive. This intelligence is amenable to suggestion from us.

You are a part of nature and of this intelligence that is greater than any single individual. The individual you are is also a particularized form of this intelligence. This infinite power is in all things and all space, and it will manifest from the spiritual or formless energy that is in the unseen world into the world of form and boundaries.

When we know this beyond a doubt, and put it into practice in our lives, we will see the pictures of our hearts' desires transformed into our outer reality. The fifth principle explains the importance of our feeling absolutely worthy of receiving these gifts.

HONORING YOUR WORTHINESS
TO RECEIVE

——————————— ☯ ☯ ☯   *The Fifth Principle*

*I*n order to become a manifester, literally taking part in the process of co-creating your life and attracting to yourself the objects of your heart's desires, you must know that you are worthy of receiving. This will mean examining the attitudes that you knowingly and unknowingly hold about your life. Your thoughts, which are the architects of the foundation of your material world, are what you want to examine.

Manifesting involves using the power of your inner world to craft a fuller relationship with life and attract to you what you desire. You can remind yourself all day long that the same power that brought anything into the physical world also brought you, but if you do not feel worthy, you will disrupt the natural flow of energy into your life and create a blockage that makes manifestation impossible.

The fifth principle reminds you that you are worthy of abundance. If your thoughts are based on an image of unworthiness for any reason at all, you will manifest what those thoughts impart to the universal mind. The energy described in the fourth principle will align with what it is that you radiate. "As a man thinks, so is he," are not empty words. They state a basic truth of how the universe works.

Thinking that abundance is incompatible with spirituality is a myth that influences many of us and is the largest impediment there is to feeling worthy.

SELFISH?

The myth that abundance and spirituality are incompatible is fueled by thoughts that it is selfish and improper to visualize and desire material things. Let's examine this attitude and determine if you have been influenced into believing it to be your truth.

Take a look around your world and notice the abundance and endlessness of our universe. It goes on and on, beyond our ability to imagine its vastness. This abundance flows from the same energy that comprises our fundamental essence. It is you. You are it. Make no mistake about it.

Material form is how spirit makes itself known to us while we are in form ourselves. Spirit manifests in trees, oceans, fish, birds, minerals, vegetables, flowers and you. All that you see around you is a part of the material manifestation of spirit. Matter is not an illusion, or something that ought not to be, but is the necessary means through which spirit differentiates itself on this plane of existence.

To feel that it is selfish or non-spiritual to desire and manifest is to divide the world of spirit and the world of matter into polar opposites. When we adopt an attitude of spirit being incompatible with matter, we are denying the spirit that is in matter as its originating energy. We also deny the validity of ourselves as spiritual beings.

There is no reason to feel ashamed of wanting things to come into your life. It is far better to have an attitude of deserving whatever shows up in your life and to be willing to participate in the dance of creation as a co-creator. When we shift to seeing that together they comprise one harmonious whole, we remove the stigma of selfishness. Just as each of us is one harmonious whole comprised of spirit and matter, so, too, is the entire universe.

The process of life taking form is a mystery. That mystery is governed by a creative energy that is knowable when we genuinely feel worthy of receiving its blessings in form. Abundance is the way of the creative force in the universe. You are entitled to have abundance in your life, and to radiate prosperity to all that you encounter in your world. Nothing is gained by making yourself small and insignificant other than to manifest smallness and insignificance in your life.

To facilitate an attitude of deserving abundance, it will be helpful to examine what you want to change in order to cultivate this knowing at the cellular level of your being.

THE CORE COMPONENTS OF WORTHINESS

Everything that you need to master in order to make this fifth principle a working model in your life is available as a mental activity. You do not need to go out into the world and conquer it in any way. It is simply a matter of changing your mind about your basic worthiness to receive all of God's blessings, be they material or otherwise.

There has been a lot of effort put into conditioning us to feel unworthy of having all that life has to offer. Most of us have accepted a lot of the stuff that egos have thrown our way, beginning with our arrival as infants. Certainly there is nothing wrong with an attitude of poverty and asceticism. If this is your path, you know it deep within yourself and you know that God appears in all things material and nonmaterial. Spirit cannot be divided into better or worse, depending on which of God's creations you opt to have or not have in your life.

Feeling worthy of any blessings or desires is a feature of your inner life. To remove the stigma of materialistic selfishness you may need to rearrange your inner perceptions. Here are the major perceptions of beings who know they are worthy and deserving of all of God's blessing.

1: *My self-esteem comes from myself.* This person's statement of his or her inner perception might be something like the following: "As a child of God, my worthiness is a given. I am not divided into spirit and body, rather, I am a part of the all-knowing creation called God itself. I am a human expressing God without reservation or restraint."

One of the reasons children are often able to express genius is because they have not yet been hypnotized by the idea of being limited. If they are able to resist this hypnotic spell, they remain geniuses and are able to express their unlimited selves throughout their lives on earth.

Too often the ideas of other egos are what constitute our impressions of ourselves as unworthy. We listen to the admonitions of others who have low self-regard, and who are attempting to exert influence and power over us. We then take on the external validations of our unworthiness and begin to see ourselves as some significant others would have us believe we are. It is beyond the scope of most young children to resist these ideas. But, as adults, we can look back at this hypnosis and free ourselves from its absurdity.

You must know within that you are a part of the light that lighteth every man. You are evidence of the existence of God, and in your own particularized individuality, you have God within you. Therefore, you must be able to say with conviction, "God is me, and I am God." It is this truth that will free you from your feelings of unworthiness to attract to yourself all that you desire.

Think of your own desires to manifest as having been placed there by spirit, and that those desires, which are housed in love and service, are precisely what God wants to give you, and that your desire is the direct path to receiving those blessings. Let go of the idea that desire is selfishness and remind yourself that if you had no desires ever, you would still be living an infantile existence with toys in a sandbox.

Whenever you feel unworthy of having your manifestations arrive, remind yourself that no one is unworthy and that the same divine energy that flows through you flows through all of God's children and that all are worthy. This includes you.

Your desires are the very tools that allow you to grow and experience the perfection of the universe. They take you beyond any limitations that you might have embraced and lead you to a higher spiritual awareness. Even the idea of achieving enlightenment and mastery is a desire that you must honor.

2: *I accept myself without complaint.* A person with this self-perception thinks something like the following: "I am willing to face everything about myself, without lapsing into self-contempt or repudiating my essential value as a piece of God."

Self-acceptance is something that must be unconditionally known within ourselves. To accept oneself is not necessarily to accept every behavior. Rather, it is a refusal to engage in sabotaging acts of self-loathing. If you are in a state of self-rejection you cannot feel worthy of the munificence of the universe. Your inner energy is centered on what is wrong with yourself and with complaining to yourself and anyone who will listen.

You showed up here in a specific body, with certain physical characteristics, with certain measurements and with certain parents and siblings. This is your reality for the physical plane, and it requires a high degree of willingness to look at your physical appearance and say, "I accept this without complaint."

If you are unwilling to make such a declaration, your inner energy will be sapped by anger, guilt, fear and pain, all combining to circumvent the possibility of manifesting your desires. Remember, the ability to attract to yourself is based on the idea, "That which ought to be . . . is already." What you desire is already here and can only flow into your immediate life if you are open to it doing so. Those thoughts of self-repudiation guarantee that you cannot put out into the universe the knowing and loving energy that is going to work for you.

Self-acceptance is nothing more than a shift in consciousness. It requires only a change of mind. If your hair is falling out, then you have the choice to mask it, worry about it or accept it. Acceptance means that you really have to do nothing. You honor your body and the divine intelligence that is at work. When someone else implies that you have a problem because your hair is falling out, you don't even know how to relate to their observation. Acceptance removes the label of "problem."

This is not a faked attitude. It is merely removing the ego from your inner assessments, which are centered on the approval of others. With self-acceptance you are able to honestly say, "I am what I am and I accept it." Once this attitude is firmly in place from a position of self-honesty, your worthiness to receive the gifts of the universe becomes aligned with that divine power.

Self-repudiation causes a misalignment with your divinity. Only you can make the shift. It is nothing more than an inner perception that you have the power to change in this very instant.

3: *I take full responsibility for my life and what it is and is not.* This involves a removal of our strong ego-dominated inclination to cast blame on others for what is absent from our lives. Taking total responsibility means an awareness of the power that is inherent within yourself.

Rather than saying "They made me the way I am today" you shift your inner thought to "I chose to be passive and fearful around other people." This goes for every single facet of your personality and life circumstances.

To be willing to accept total responsibility for yourself puts you in a position of being worthy of receiving and attracting the object of your desires.

If someone else is responsible for your perceived shortcomings, and you are blaming them for these troubles, then you are also saying that in order to manifest your heart's desire you need to have the permission of those others. This act of abdicating responsibility destroys your ability to empower yourself to higher levels of awareness.

When you know that you are responsible for how you chose to react to every life situation, and that you are essentially alone within yourself at all moments, then you can very privately put out into the universe that which you want to bring to yourself. However, blaming others for your life situations shifts the power to those you believe are responsible for creating the circumstances.

I have a private inner dialogue with the universe about the circumstances that show up in my life. I come from the position that there are absolutely no accidents and that everything that occurs in my life has a lesson attached to it, and that I brought it into my life. Regardless of how absurd or inconsequential it might seem, I say to myself, "Why did I create this in this moment?"

Thus, if I am having a negative thought and at the same moment I bump my head on a cupboard door, I say, "What was I thinking at that moment?" and I take full responsibility for correcting those negative thoughts and for the bump that reminded me to correct that kind of thinking. I do the same when I am writing. If I feel inclined to go to the mailbox before writing, I follow that inner signal and often find an article in the mail that clarifies a point that was fuzzy. I take responsibility for knowing that what I needed was there and that my inner voices of intuition were guiding me.

This little game serves me in the sense of taking full responsibility for my life and eradicating the inclination to blame other people or circumstances. I trust in this inner knowledge. I rely on seemingly coincidental happenings and I know that I am responsible for all of it. As this sense of responsibility has grown, I find it impossible to blame anyone for anything in my life, from the most inconsequential things, such as bumping or cutting myself, or others not showing up on time, to major life disappointments and my relationships with my wife and the rest of my family; for all of it I assume total responsibility.

I trust in the divine wisdom that is particularized in me that allows these things to transpire. I refuse to question the wisdom or to blame bad luck or to credit good luck. I see it all as a part of my own functioning in the universe, without complaint.

The willingness to be responsible without complaining puts you into the natural flow of all divine energy. It keeps you from having to fight the world, allowing you to go with it. Everything that you complain about puts you in a position of figuratively having to take arms against it and fight. Everything that you need to fight weakens you, while that which you are for empowers you.

I am asking you to be *for* yourself. With an attitude of self-responsibility, you will notice that the heavens are exceedingly cooperative. Getting the heavens to cooperate means getting yourself out of a complaining mind-set and into one of total self-responsibility.

4: *I do not choose to accept guilt into my life.* This mind-set creates thoughts such as: "I will not use up the precious currency of my life, my present moments, immobilized with guilt over what happened in the past."

This statement requires you to know the difference between a) genuine regret and learning from the past; and b) remaining in a state of reproach or guilt today. Learning from one's mistakes and taking corrective action are spiritually and psychologically sound practices. You did it, you didn't like the way you felt afterward, so you decide not to repeat the behavior. That is not guilt. Guilt is when you continue to feel immobilized and depressed; those feelings keep you from living effectively in the present.

When you are filled with guilt, your energy is awash with anguish and self-reproach. You are so down on yourself that you feel unworthy of receiving blessings from the universe or anyone in it. Persistent feelings of guilt will prevent you from manifesting anything worthwhile because you are attracting the very same things that you are putting out to the universe. More anguish, more reasons to feel bad, and more evidence to prove that you are not worth what you desire.

When you put past behaviors into a context of learning from them and moving on, regardless of how horrible they may seem to you, you clear yourself of the negativity surrounding these actions. Forgiving yourself means that you are able to extend love to yourself even when your perceived shortcomings are painfully evident to you.

Once you learn this valuable lesson, you seek God's forgiveness, too. But if you continue to harbor the pain internally you will feel unworthy of God's forgiveness and consequently will be unable to accept any of your divine rights as a child of God.

No matter what you do not particularly love about yourself, including your behaviors and your appearance, to be successful at manifesting, you need to love yourself in spite of your perceived flaws. For example, if you are chronically overweight, or addicted, your internal sentences of guilt sound something like this: "I am really going to love myself when I am finally a normal weight" or "I will truly value myself as a worthwhile human being when I am finally over this addiction once and for all."

These are the sentences of guilt that reinforce an attitude of unworthiness and inhibit the manifestation process. These internal sentences need to be shifted to: "I love myself while I am overweight. I am not this weight in the first place and I refuse to think of myself in self-degrading terms regardless of the condition of my body. I am love, and I extend this love to all of me." The same kind of inner programming must take place for addictions or anything else that you feel guilty about.

There are 483,364 words in *A Course in Miracles*. The word "beware" appears only once: "Beware of the temptation to see yourself as unfairly treated." The warning speaks to removing guilt and taking responsibility for one's life. By removing the inclination to wallow in self-reproach, we also remove the idea that by suffering in the present moment we will redeem ourselves and can pay for our sins with guilt. Life doesn't work this way. Your suffering keeps you in a state of fear and immobilization. That is not a solution to handling your life problems.

There is a solution, and that solution is in loving yourself, and in trusting in God that your "shortcomings" are nothing more than lessons leading you to a new spiritual level. By refusing to buy into the conditioned notion that guilt is good and you deserve to feel guilty, and that guilt will help you pay for your sins, you reinforce the idea that you are worthy of any desires of yours that you want to manifest in your life.

5: *I understand the importance of having harmony between my thoughts, my feelings and my behavior.* To the extent that you remain incongruent in any of these three areas of thinking, feeling or behaving, you will impede the process of heightened awareness and the ability to manifest your heart's desire.

This is the last of the five points that contribute to your feelings of worthiness about receiving God's munificence in your life. It is also the most significant because it defines your level of integrity. To have thoughts about how you would like to conduct your life and to posit these thoughts as your essential way of being, and then to feel guilty, fearful, anxious or anything else as a result of not living up to these inner positions results in addictive, manipulative and self-defeating behavior.

To be congruent you must be honest about your own thoughts. It is crucial to examine your thoughts and forthrightly proclaim what it is that you choose to know internally. Even if this is perceived as a shortcoming by everyone else, if you are honest with yourself you will find that your emotional reactions will be consistent with your inner world.

You will feel peaceful and content, and this will be apparent in your behavior. This is true for virtually everything about your life. Your thoughts about health, relationships, prosperity, God, work, recreation, whatever. If these thoughts are rooted in love and you honestly know that you are here to express love, kindness and forgiveness toward yourself, toward your work and co-workers, toward the money you receive, toward your spiritual beliefs, then you will be in harmony and you will welcome the blessings that result from your personal conduct in these matters.

However, if you embrace these thoughts yet fail to act on them in the daily working of your life, you will feel incongruent and, consequently, you will not feel that you are deserving of desires being fulfilled.

Addictive behavior will continue in your life if you remain incongruent. All unhealthy eating habits will continue if you remain incongruent. All scarcity perceptions will remain if you remain incongruent. These are strong statements, yet they reflect a consciousness that you must grasp if you want to change your status from being unworthy to being worthy.

You do not have to adopt any particular spiritual practice or set of beliefs. You have to, however, create a sense of congruency within yourself to be able to attain this state of worthiness, which is a prerequisite for the manifestation process. When you are being eaten up inside, in your own private corner of awareness that is not available to anyone else other than God, you will behave in self-defeating ways that verify your lack of inner congruity.

By being honest with yourself about what you believe, and then acting on that principle regardless of what others might think or say, you promote an inner peace that gives you a strong sense of worthiness. I encourage you to examine your thoughts carefully in all areas of your life, and identify where you are not in harmony with your actions. Then work each day to bring about more of a sense of inner congruence that meets with your own personal standards, and keep this a private matter.

You will find the behaviors that you dislike beginning to disappear and that you are promoting a sense of balance that gives you peace. There is nothing your highest self wants more than peace. This peace makes you feel worthy of all of God's richest blessings, and when you radiate this out into the world, it is returned to you without fail.

These five attitudes provide you with the tools for creating an inner atmosphere of worthiness. They all reflect an ability to live peacefully in the present moment and to discard many of the attitudes of your past that keep you in a constant state of feeling powerless and unworthy of being able to manifest more blessings and happiness into your life. Often this feeling persists because you are locked into the story of your earlier wounds. To finalize the path of worthiness, you must sever your relationship to these old wounds.

UNBONDING YOURSELF FROM YOUR PAST WOUNDS

The inclination to bond to our wounds rather than move past them traps us in a constant state of feeling unworthy. A person who has experienced traumatic events in life, such as sexual abuse, the death of loved ones, traumatic illnesses, accidents, family disruption, drug addictions and the like, can become bonded with the past painful events and replay them for attention or pity. These wounds of our lives can seem to give us an enormous amount of power over others.

The more we tell others about our wounds and our suffering, the more we create an atmosphere of pity for ourselves. Our creative spirit remains so connected to our memories of woundedness that it cannot be about the business of transforming and manifesting. A feeling of being unworthy of receiving all that one desires is the result.

Very often the tale of these woes is told in the first few moments with a sort of urgency for the listener to know how horrible the wounding was and still is. After a while the ego uses this energy as a power play in individual and group situations that encourage discussion of one's struggle to survive the wounding. This can keep individuals from advancing spiritually and can reinforce the image of themselves as unfortunate.

The tendency to bond with the wounds of our lives reminds us of how unworthy we are of receiving anything that we really would like because we remain in a state of suffering. The more these painful stories are recalled and repeated, the more the person is guaranteed of not attracting his or her desires.

Perhaps the most powerful sentence you can memorize in this regard is "Your biography becomes your biology." And I would add, "Your biology becomes your lack of spiritual fulfillment." By hanging onto the traumas of your earlier life, you literally have an impact on the cells of your body. When we examine the biology of an individual, we find that his or her biography is close to the surface. Thoughts of anguish, self-pity, fear, hate and the like all take their toll on the body and the spirit. After a while, the body is unable to heal, largely because of these thoughts.

Attachment to early pain comes from a mythological perception of "I am entitled to a perfect, pain-free childhood. Anything that interferes with this perception I will use for the rest of my life. Telling my story will be my power." What the perception does is give an injured child inside you permission to control you for the rest of your life. Moreover, it provides a strong sense of illusory power.

The moment anyone stands up to you, or crosses you, or even disagrees with you, the injury is brought forth with accusations of insensitivity concerning the other's treatment of you. This power is empty, however, because it continuously reinforces the idea that you are not worthy of being free from these events. The unworthiness then inhibits you from attracting to yourself the love, kindness and abundance that is the universe.

This is not to say that one ought not to deal with traumas and help them to heal. But it is to say that one must be very careful to avoid explaining present life in terms of traumatic history. The painful events in our lives are like a raft you use to cross the river. You must remember to get off on the other side.

Notice your body when it is wounded. An open

wound actually closes quite quickly. Just imagine what it would be like if that wound remained open for a long time. It would become infected and ultimately would kill the entire organism. The closing up of a wound and allowing it to heal can work the same way in your inner world of thoughts.

So, don't lead with your injuries. Deal with them and ask family and friends to be compassionate while you are grieving or recuperating. Then, ask them to kindly remind you when it has taken on the form of a predictable response. Perhaps four or five times your friends and loved ones will say, "You did suffer a tragic experience and I can truly empathize with you and your need to discuss it. I care, and I'll listen and offer help if that is what you want." Then, after several such interchanges, ask your friends to gently remind you to not repeat the story for the purpose of gaining power through pity.

When you go backward and continuously relive your pain, including describing it in most introductions and labeling yourself (incest survivor, alcoholic, orphan, abandoned), you do not do so for strength. You do it because of your inner experience of bitterness. This bitterness shows itself in hatred and anger as you discuss these events, and you are literally feeding the cell tissue of your life from this harvest of past events.

This continues to infect the body and prevent healing. And so it is with the spirit. This harvest of bitterness keeps you from feeling worthy. You begin to cultivate an image of being dirty, unlucky, unworthy and maligned, and this is what you send out into the universe, which will inhibit any sense of attracting love and bliss into your life.

The way out of bonding to your wounds is through forgiveness. Forgiveness is the most powerful thing that you can do for your physiology and your spirituality, and it remains one of the least attractive things to us, largely because our egos rule so unequivocally. To forgive is somehow associated with saying that it is all right, that we accept the evil deed. But this is not forgiveness.

Forgiveness means that you fill yourself with love and you radiate that love outward and refuse to hang onto the venom or hatred that was engendered by the behaviors that caused the wounds. Forgiveness is a spiritual act of love for yourself and it sends a message to everyone, including yourself, that you are an object of love and that that is what you are going to impart.

This is the process of unbonding from those wounds and no longer hanging onto them as prized possessions. It means letting go of the language of blame and self-pity and no longer leading with one's wounds and injuries from the past. It means privately forgiving and not asking anyone else to understand. It means leaving behind the eye-for-an-eye attitude that only makes for more pain and the need for more revenge, and replacing it with an attitude of love and forgiveness. The spiritual literature available to us from all religious persuasions honors this way.

Feeling worthy is essential to being able to attract to yourself what you desire. It is simply a matter of common sense. If you don't feel that you deserve something, why would the divine energy that is in all things send it your way? Thus, you must shift to knowing that you and the divine energy are one and the same, and that it is your ego that is conniving to keep you from knowing the power of this in your own life.

Listed below are some of the major attitudes and behaviors that you can incorporate into your consciousness to facilitate the growth of your feelings of worthiness.

A PLAN FOR ADOPTING AND HONORING YOUR WORTHINESS TO RECEIVE AND ATTRACT FROM THE DIVINE SOURCE

The following suggestions represent a step-by-step plan to assist your receptivity to the power of manifesting in your life. If put into practice, there will be no doubt of your feeling worthy of the beneficence of the divine, all-embracing spirit.

⊙ The word "inspiration" literally means "to be infused with spirit." In spirit, if you will.

⊙ Practice doing what you love and loving what you do each day. If you are going to do something, then give yourself the benefit of not complaining about it and, instead, loving the activity. Your theme here is "I love what I do and I do what I love." This puts you "in spirit" and literally provides you with the enthusiasm for being a worthy recipient of God's grace. The word enthusiasm comes from the Greek root *entheos,* literally, "to be filled with God."

⊘ Make every effort to remove internal habits of pessimism, negativity, judgment, complaints, gossip, cynicism, resentment and fault-finding from your vocabulary and your inner dialogue. Replace these with optimism, love, acceptance, kindness and peace as your way of processing your world and the people in it.

⊘ Regardless of how much you may be tempted to go back to the cynical habits, remind yourself that this is the energy that you are putting out into the world, and it sends a message of blockage to the energy that would return what you desire to you. If you are filled with negativity, you are out of balance and your resentments indicate that you do not feel worthy or ready to accept the loving energy that you desire.

⊘ Give yourself quiet time each day to erase feelings of unworthiness. This time of prayer or meditation or just experiencing silence will nourish your soul and will eventually remove any doubts about you not deserving to be the beneficiary of the universe's abundance.

⊘ Read spiritual literature and poetry, and listen to soothing classical music whenever possible. I have

found that simply reading the poetry of Walt
Whitman, or Rabindranath Tagore, or Rumi puts
everything into a more sacred perspective for me.

☉ It is like doing one's spiritual homework to read
the great teachings of the masters, including the
New Testament, *A Course in Miracles,* the Torah,
the Koran, the Bhagavad Gita. These great works
are a way to become in spirit (inspired) and to
dissolve doubts about your deserving to materialize in your life what you desire.

☉ This beautiful poem from Kahlil Gibran's *The
Prophet* is an example of such literature. I include
it here for you to study. Pay particular attention
to the words "Your hearts know in silence the
secrets of the days and nights" and "For the soul
walks upon all paths." These are the thoughts I
have been emphasizing throughout this book in
encouraging you to know your own divine worthiness.

On Self-Knowledge

from *The Prophet* by Kahlil Gibran
(1923)

And a man said, Speak to us on self-knowledge.
And he answered, saying:
Your hearts know in silence the secrets of
the days and nights.

But your ears thirst for the sound
    of your hearts' knowledge.
You would know in words that which
    you would have always known
    in thought.
You would touch with your fingers
    the naked body of your dreams.

And it is well you should.
The hidden well-spring of your soul must
    needs rise and run
    murmuring to the sea;
And the treasure of your infinite depths
    would be revealed to your eyes.
But let there be no scales to weigh your
    unknown treasure;
And seek not the depths of your knowledge
    with staff or
    sounding line.
For self is a sea boundless and measureless.

Say not, "I have found the truth," but rather,
"I have found a truth."
Say not, "I have found the path of the soul."
Say rather, "I have met the soul walking
    upon my path."
For the soul walks upon all paths.
The soul walks not upon a line, neither does
    it grow like a reed.
The soul unfolds itself, like a lotus of
    countless petals.

⊙ Allow yourself to be surrounded by things of beauty as much as possible.

I am writing these words on Marco Island in southwest Florida. Each evening I leave my typewriter and go out to the beach and experience the magnificence of the sun setting over the Gulf of Mexico. Each time I participate in this daily ritual I am filled with awe at the enormous energy that is involved in moving the earth once more in its orbital relationship to the sun. I breathe in this energy and feel thankful for being a part of all this beauty.

To be a part of this sunset each evening fills me with a sense of a home beyond this planet and opens me up to the deeper nature within myself. I could never feel unworthy of the grace and munificence of the universe when I am immersed in such beauty. It is the same with virtually any experience of beauty—it has a tendency to remove the doubt about your own divinity and connection to the ultimate truth that is in everything and everyone.

⊙ Practice kindness toward yourself and others as frequently as possible.

Give up your need to be right and win in favor of being kind and you will soon know the bliss of inner peace. Remember, it is your highest self that only wants peace. When you are practicing kindness, peace shows up right on schedule. When you are at peace with yourself and your world, you know that you are a worthy recipient of all that comes your way. You begin to trust in the energy that brings the fulfillment of your desires.

When you are in turmoil and consequently preoccupied with winning and defeating, you are at the mercy of your ego, which loves the confusion. All of the inner confusion keeps you wondering about yourself and your own value in comparison to others. This brings in the doubt about your worthiness to receive and manifest.

Make it your own special mission to be kind to others each day at least once, and to extend the same privilege to yourself as much as possible. You always have a choice in how your inner self is going to react. The choice of guilt, worry, fear or judgment is nothing more than a thought transferred to your physiology. When your physical self is imbalanced with these emotions, you become too sick and too unhappy to even think about participating in the act of co-creating a blissful life. You sabotage yourself, and all because of an unwillingness to be kind to yourself and to others.

⊙ Begin to process the universe as a friendly rather than an unfriendly place. Place all of your wounds from the earlier stages of your life into the category "Lessons for Life." Stop leading with those wounds and making them your badge of identification.

Disengage yourself from the attitude of this being an evil world filled with evil people, and, beginning today, look for the good in people you meet. Remember, for every act of evil there are a million acts of kindness. This universe runs on the energy of harmony and balance. Breathe in that energy and breathe out those ideas of your being life's victim. All of the attachment to your traumas creates a cellular toxicity in your body, and a spiritual poisoning of your soul.

🕐 Say it over and over until it registers: "I am what I am and I am worthy of the abundance that is the universe and all that is in it, including me."

You are now on a path of knowing you are worthy of attracting and manifesting in your world. You are aware of your highest self. You trust in yourself and the divine wisdom that created you. You know that you are not separate from your environment and that the power to attract is within you.

The next principle involves the energy of love and how important it is to know and experience it in all of your being before you begin applying the last three principles of manifestation.

Mira Bai knows that to find the Divine One
The only indispensable is Love.
                    —MIRA BAI

CONNECTING TO THE DIVINE SOURCE
WITH UNCONDITIONAL LOVE

—————————— ☽ ☽ ☽ *The Sixth Principle*

There is no greater power in heaven or on earth
than pure, unconditional love. This is the heart of the
sixth principle of manifestation.

The nature of the God force, that unseen intelligence in all things, which causes the material world
and is the center of both the spiritual and physical
plane, is best described as pure, unconditional love. It
is the glue that holds all things material in place and
keeps them from collapsing into uncountable particles. This God force is the oversoul to which we are
always connected because we are localized extensions
of that force.

You may feel infinitely worthy of attracting to yourself material and spiritual prosperity, but if you are not

living the way of unconditional love you are interfering with your ability to manifest in your life. In order to be divinely aligned with this universal infinite energy, you must become unconditional love.

Though it seems easy and even appropriate to announce, "I practice unconditional love," it is far from a reality for most of us on this physical plane. Unconditional love has eluded most of us, largely because we tend to identify it as affection or sentiment.

THE ENERGY OF LOVE DISSOLVES LIMITATIONS

When I speak of love emanating from your soul and from the divine consciousness of God, I speak of something that the lower self or the ego cannot grasp. I am not speaking about "feeling good" toward others, romantic love, showering everyone with affection or "touchy-feely" behavior. This unconditional love that I write of here is an experience of the harmony of life. It is simply too deep and too profound for our ordinary selves to activate.

This energy of unconditional love is the power behind creation. It guides all of our natural laws. This love can be imagined as a vibration that carries thought forms from one's mind into material expression. In its highest nature, love is the force that we recognize as the will of God. It is the alchemy that we embrace to make sense of how things are materialized from the world of spirit.

These are strong words, which are essential for you to know if you are to make the transition from one who takes what life presents to one who becomes a co-creator with the universal energy of unconditional love.

I suggest you embark on an experiment in which you practice only unconditional love for several days, perhaps even a week. Make this a private activity, but vow to yourself that you will only allow unconditional loving thoughts to emanate from your consciousness. Make an intense proclamation to live unconditional love for a designated period of time.

During this time refuse to have judgmental or critical thoughts. In your quiet time think only peace and love. In all of your relationships think and act in only loving ways. Extend loving thoughts and energy wherever and whenever you encounter anyone or anything. Become unconditional love for this period of time.

This practice of becoming unconditional love is a prerequisite to the manifesting process. By pouring love into your immediate environment and practicing gentleness in all of your thoughts, words and actions, your immediate circle of friends will begin responding in a whole new way. Furthermore, this act becomes expansive very quickly and you can radiate this love to your community and to people you read about in newspapers, including those who are labeled terrorists, murderers, scam artists and the like.

You emphasize the "un" in unconditional love. You become detached and loving toward all. You are not loving the hostile act, but you are loving the spirit that is blocked in those who are harmful and unloving. When you can live this way and reject all thoughts and actions that are not of an unconditionally loving nature, you will experience the essence of your spirit and know how to overcome limitations in your life.

This is a task that your conditioning will not easily encourage. But for a few days you can persevere just so you know what the divine universal spirit is like. It judges no one and no thing, it does not moralize, it does not show favoritism, it merely exists as unconditional love, radiating harmony and allowing everything and everyone to unfold. Each day millions of flowers open and then close without any force, only with the all-flowing unconditional love that is the heart of universal, infinite and eternal energy. With this exercise you are cultivating that aspect of yourself.

As you practice being unconditional love, contemplate and meditate on the sacred unconditional love that is the heart of yourself also. Imagine an atom of unconditional love that is at the very center of your existence. Feel this presence in your heart and feel it opening and radiating outward. Soon this impersonal feeling that is not dependent on anyone or anything, or any belief system, will radiate to a feeling of being connected to the infinite energy of unconditional love that is God.

With this transformation you are on the path of manifestation. You will connect by ridding yourself of all judgment, anger, moralizing, preaching, hate, rancor and all of the other various tools of the ego.

What can you expect as you practice a few days of

being total, unconditional love? If all of your meditations are devoted to love, and if you pour love into
every single situation and every single person you
meet, and beyond that to everyone on the planet and
to the infinity of the universe, you will feel yourself
becoming a different person. You will sleep more
soundly. You will feel at peace virtually all of the time.
Your relationships will be more deeply spiritual. Most
significantly, you will begin recognizing the "coincidences" of your life with greater regularity. Your
thought forms of unconditional love will begin to produce what you desire without your even being aware of
how it is happening. Your dreams will be more intense,
and the vision of your purpose will become clearer.

I am suggesting that you can love more, and
unconditionally, without expecting anything in
return; as a result, the limitations that you experience
will disappear. Try it before you reject it. There is an
oft-quoted piece from the New Testament that seems
appropriate to insert here. For me, it is one of the
most profound passages ever written. It is reproduced here from Corinthians 13, on "Love."

And now I will show you the most excellent way.

If I speak in the tongues of men and of angels,
but have not love, I am only a resounding gong
or a clanging cymbal. If I have the gift of
prophecy and can fathom all mysteries and all
knowledge, and if I have a faith that can move
mountains, but have not love, I am nothing. If I

give all I possess to the poor and surrender my body to the flames, but have not love, I gain nothing.

Love is patient, love is kind. It does not envy, it does not boast, it is not proud. It is not rude, it is not self seeking, it is not easily angered, it keeps no record of wrong. Love does not delight in evil but rejoices with the truth. It always protects, always trusts, always hopes, always perseveres.

Love never fails. But where there are prophecies they will cease, where there are tongues they will be stilled, where there is knowledge, it will pass away. For we know in part and we prophesy in part. But when perfection comes, the imperfect disappears. When I was a child, I talked like a child. I thought like a child. I reasoned like a child. When I became a man, I put childish ways behind me. Now we see but a poor reflection as in a mirror, then we shall see face to face. Now I know in part, then I shall know fully, even as I am fully known.

And now these three remain; faith, hope and love.

But the greatest of these is Love.

Yes, the greatest of these is love. It will make the imperfect disappear, and it will allow you to move into that spiritually fulfilling world of co-creating your life based on the model of unconditional love.

I am well aware of the improbability of living an unconditionally loving life in all of our moments. I imagine your ego is protesting that this idea is absurd because you are only human and humans have short-comings. Nevertheless, I ask you to do this exercise for a few days or a week. You see, I know that it will become habitual when you feel the richness of your life with this new awareness.

Unconditional love is the ultimate mystery of life. It may appear simple, but it is so powerful that it will shake you free of your ego domination if you give it even a short tryout in your life. Until we learn to transcend the ego we continue to contribute to the insanity that we witness in the world. Detaching and becoming an unconditionally loving observer is the way to cultivate a healthy, balanced relationship between ego and spirit.

THE PROCESS OF DETACHED OBSERVATION

One of the great meditation exercises that I learned many years ago involves imagining lifting yourself out of your body and floating into space so far that you are actually observing the entire planet. If you do this, try to imagine what the earth is like without you on it. It is a very difficult task for your ego to even contemplate the world without you in it. Next, begin to observe the planet without any judgment, refusing to label anything as good or bad, right or wrong. Simply instruct yourself to notice, allow and send unconditional love.

You probably will find it easier to send out unconditional love when you are not there to interfere. That is, you can love unconditionally when your ego is out of the way. This is a technique that will help you to project unconditional love.

If all you are is a being of unconditional love, you are not involved in ego concerns. When you operate from this perspective you are practicing detachment in a state of gentleness, which makes you a compassionate witness toward everyone and everything you come into contact with. It is magical to be able to extend this kind of consciousness beyond your form. This is the resolution of that great mystery of how to connect to and know God. That is, not to know about God, but *to know God*.

The process of being a detached observer occurs in the silence of your contemplations or meditations. Begin by seeking out time to be quiet and enter this inner place of love. It is in that silence that you will come to truly know this divine energy of unconditional love.

Most people in the western world have a great deal of difficulty with any prolonged periods of silence. They fill those moments with music, conversation, radio and television and anything else they can use to avoid the silence. Our culture is a noisy culture.

When I attempt to meditate and just observe the silence, I deal with vacuums, power mowers, tree trimmers, portable leaf blowers, edgers and the many machines that move earth and sand, bulldoze, clean and on and on. All of these noise machines have power sources that pollute the world with loud noise. It takes practice to learn to transcend this by going within and screening out the noise pollution. The noisy world will still filter into quiet time unless you can get far enough into nature to avoid it.

Our preoccupation with noise satisfies the ego's need to escape the serenity and unconditional love of the divine intelligence that is God. But you can become a detached observer if you make the choice to simply remove your ego from the story line and allow your higher self to take over. Become an unconditionally loving observer rather than an ego-involved participant.

Let go of your inclination to judge and moralize and take personally what you notice. Simply become the noticer. You are then aligning yourself with God, allowing all to bask in his loving blessing instead of the ego frantically insisting that there is a superior way. Being godly means expressing the love that is within you. It is much more than simply being close to it. You must be it in oneness with the universal being of God.

WHAT IT MEANS TO BE IN ONENESS

What has come to be referred to as "the will of God" is an invention of man to gain control over others. If you are convinced that there is a God's will that is separate from you, then those who claim they know God's will can dominate and control you. If you adopt this belief system, then you fall into the trap of "his will versus my will." You want to do certain things, but the "will of God" dictates otherwise.

Unconditional love and becoming a co-creator in your life is possible when you know that God is not separate from you. You and God are one and the same. In the New Testament Jesus says to the multitudes, ". . . I have said ye are Gods," and later, "When a man believes in me, he does not believe in me only, but in the one who sent me. When he looks at me he sees the one who sent me." (John, 10:34; 12:44)

What it means to be in a state of oneness is that you know the unconditional love that God has for all of creation is also the unconditional love that can be you, if you make that choice. Your free will is your freedom to embrace any thought that you desire. This free will is your gift from God. Use this free will in a spirit of love that has no conditions imposed on it.

The love that God has for you is without condition. There is no restriction or censorship placed on this love granted to you by the divine creator. You have complete freedom to do as you will, for your will and God's will are one and the same. You have the freedom to choose your thoughts within this grand scheme of unconditional love.

If it is the same as God's love for you, then you are living unconditional oneness. If you place restrictions on that love, or withhold it dependent on your judgments and hatreds, then you make it a conditional love and remove yourself from the possibility of co-creating with God. You are in conflict with the divine essence that is God. This conflicted state is nothing more than the imposition of conditions on your ability to love.

Suppose that God decided to withdraw his unconditional love from you and the world and conditions were placed upon everything. In this kind of world the people in it would have to function without freedom of thought and expression. The entire cosmos would collapse in an instant.

Life flows with the freedom of unconditional love. This is the very essence of life. No deity demands that you think a certain way or you will be cursed and destroyed. In our world we have unconditional freedom for our thoughts to be what they are. That is how you are loved. That is your gift from the divine creator, expressed through your individuality. Take that freedom away and you are no longer a human being. You lose your humanity when you lose the unconditional love that allows you to think as you choose.

Now suppose that you are able to function in the same unconditionally loving way, simply allowing yourself to be without judgment. What if you have no hatred and only extend the freedom to choose to others? You would be experiencing what is called "oneness." Your will and God's will would not be in conflict.

The conflicts that you experience are from the ego. Your ego is the idea you carry around of your separateness from God and all of God's creations. This ego needs to be reminded of its superiority over others. Thus conflict is created. But you do not have to participate in this folly. Your highest self only wants peace and is unconditional love.

Use this love for the purpose of co-creation. Every moment that you create by radiating unconditionally loving thoughts is a reflection of the same love that was responsible for your creation. Creating (or manifesting) is the act of bringing unconditional love from within your being into a form that we call the world of the concrete. In this sense, then, unconditional love can be thought of as the power to participate in the act of co-creation.

UNCONDITIONAL LOVE AS POWER

Those who seem to have the gift of attracting to themselves all manner of good things in their lives are said to be empowered in some mysterious way. The ability to reach a higher state of being, where there seems to be almost no delay between the creation of a thought form and having that thought form "show up," can be viewed in terms of unconditional love and an absence of demanding from or judging the world.

This is a power that I know is possible for each of us when we begin to adopt these basic principles of spiritual manifestation. Most of us simply do not recognize how truly powerful we are by virtue of our own ability to create thoughts, and out of these thoughts attract to ourselves the abundance of the universe. When we think rationally about this power we immediately think of the conflict between having a free will and having a destiny. This conflict often obviates the need within us to think and live in unconditionally loving ways. Our rational left brain says, "If it is already determined,

then I have no free will, and therefore anything I think
has been predetermined, so I am doomed."

Let's take a quick look at this matter of destiny,
since it is in the title of this book, and put it into a different context. *Destiny is not preordained.* Destiny is
ordained totally by you. Every single moment of your
NOW existence is the result of your previous thought.
The idea that everything is already laid out for you in
advance is a hallucination. You can and do manifest
your own destiny.

Your free will is your gift of unconditional love.
You create your destiny with this free will, and when
you venture off the path of unconditional love, you
are simply living an illusion. The illusion is that the
thoughts that you have of your separateness from
God's will put you into an obsequious position, that
God is something you must fight or fear. Obviously, if
this were true, God could not at the same time be all
loving.

Once this illusion takes hold, you become a victim
of life rather than a co-creator within it. You lose your
ability to extend the unconditional love that is your
beingness, and instead project your conditioned ego.
In other words, you give up your power to be at one
with the God force that created you, and you lose your
power to manifest or co-create the life that you desire.
Life is in conflict with your higher power.

You begin to fear this higher power and act in
servile ways toward it. You become disenchanted with
your own ability to attract anything positive and you
feel weak and powerless. You have lost the joy and

ecstasy that is the accompaniment to a life of unconditional love.

KNOWING THE JOY OF UNCONDITIONAL LOVE

The most important thing that you will gain from cultivating unconditional love will be freedom from hate and violence. When these thoughts are removed, you discover the presence of joy and peace. This is an automatic reaction to unconditional love, because you are in harmony with the creative source.

One of the lessons that you will be unlearning as you gain access to unconditional love is the mistaken belief that joy is of the ego and misery is of the spirit. The truth lies in reversing this supposition and getting to the source of spiritual joy. Simplistically stated, experiencing joy, from the point of view of the ego, is always getting what we want, and being spiritual is associated with meditating, being generous, extending kindness to others. The path to true joy and bliss in your life is affirming the spirit and subordinating the ego.

Saying to yourself that the ego is an illusion provides you with a powerful tool for manifesting. The ego identifies you as primarily a physical body, separate from God, and in need of constant stroking to massage your self-importance. When you simply say this is an illusion and it doesn't really exist, those ideas are replaced with unconditional love, and the joy that you experience is really the denial of the false and an affirmation of the truth of your being.

You are absolutely free when you are not consumed with your self-importance. You are free when you no longer need to be stroked, coddled and approved of by everyone you meet. You are free when you are no longer offended by the actions of others. Freedom allows you to extend your inner self to the outer world, and that is love.

There is a great sense of joy in feeling free. Think of times when you have felt the freest in your life. When the pressures to perform are off. When you are walking in nature. When no one is badgering you to meet deadlines. When you are in solitude and communing with God. If you have made the connection to your inner life, these are the most joyful times. When you are experiencing this kind of joyful freedom, you feel inspired, and, of course, this means that you are "in spirit."

The most creative times of my own life are when I allow myself to be free. This freedom produces a great joy within me that manifests as new ideas to expand my work and be more purposeful, to be a better writer, teacher, father and husband, to share this love that I feel with all who care to know about it.

Joy, freedom and unconditional love are inseparable; they flow from the experience of each other. To be joyful is to hold onto nothing and to have no restrictions. This is also the feeling of freedom, and it is a result of embracing the unconditional love of the divine energy that is the center of your being.

Authentic joy is not merely the pleasure of the moment. These ego pleasures are fleeting and transient. They demand more, just like a drug, in an attempt to be fulfilled. But fulfillment is mostly an illusion with fleeting pleasures. All of the pleasures of the body are not evil, they are simply temporary.

This is not to say that one ought not to enjoy a massage, a delicious meal, lovemaking and all of the pleasures of the body. But, that one should know that true joy is not in the bodily pleasure. It is in the mind, which is processing and allowing you to experience the pleasure; the body is simply neutral, as are all *things*. It is the mind that makes it real, not the reverse.

The body cannot make us real any more than it can heal the mind. Nor does the body, in and of itself, give us joy. It is in the mind that the healing of the body originates, and it is in the mind where joy also originates. Your purpose is to align your mind with the unconditional love that is the divine source of all material things, including your body. That source is love. With that alignment comes joy and power.

When one drop of water separates from the ocean it becomes a speck that is, essentially, powerless and weak and unable to sustain itself. But, when it aligns with its source, the ocean itself, it is powerful beyond what is possible as an individual drop of ocean. So it is with you. Alone, separated from your divine source, you are a skin-encapsulated ego living the illusion that you are important and powerful. But, realigned, you know the joy that comes from this partnership. And what you are aligning with is pure, unconditional love and acceptance of all that is. You abandon your fear of anything.

UNCONDITIONAL LOVE AS
AN ABSENCE OF FEAR

All fears stem from the idea that we are alone and separated from the one divine source that we give many names to, including God or Holy Spirit. When you adopt a stance of unconditional love, you automatically abandon fear. In the absence of fear and in the presence of unconditional love you find the solution to the mystery of manifestation. Once you truly know that you are not separate or alone, fear is replaced by unconditional love and you have gained access to the Holy Spirit.

The ego is where fears originate, with constant messages that you are incomplete and need more, that you need to win to be better in comparison to others. With its unceasing pressure, the ego keeps you in a constant state of turmoil and anxiety. Here is where all fears are birthed and nurtured within you.

To accept unconditional love as your premise for living, you will have to tell the ego that there is no need to prove anything and that all you want or hope for is already here. The ego, moreover, needs to be taught that you are connected to a creative source that is far more powerful than the ego.

You are able to detach from how it has to show up, and you can send out the energy of unconditional love with your thoughts wherever you go, trusting that it is all in order. No demands, no pressure. A simple knowing accompanied by an unconditionally loving attitude. With this kind of declaration, fear is removed from your life and is replaced with love. Remember the biblical quote, "Perfect love casteth out all fear."

Fear and love are unable to reside simultaneously within you. If you are afraid, you have cast out love. If you are experiencing perfect love, which is within your free will, then you have cast out fear.

This principle of unconditional love as a prerequisite to manifesting your own destiny is a tough one to put into practice full-time. Yet you can begin this process by working on it one step at a time, beginning right now. Below are some suggestions for living and radiating unconditional love.

SOME WAYS OF PUTTING UNCONDITIONAL LOVE INTO PRACTICE

⊙ Keep uppermost in mind that love transforms. Every single act of love releases blocked energy in your body. Unconditional love heals the body and the mind. Keep reminding yourself of this truth until it becomes your reality. Love is a frequency that you can choose to tune into, just as you tune into a frequency on the radio.

⊙ The polarity of love is fear. Fear is a current of energy that literally runs through your body and is produced when you feel cut off from the source of unconditional love. Every time you experience fear, ask yourself, "What is going on that I have substituted fear for love in this moment?" This kind of self-talk will bring you back to an awareness that fear is running through you because you have lost your alignment with love.

In this moment of insight, send the fear energy out of your body by embracing unconditional love. In those moments of fear, your anxiety about failing, not receiving approval, your appearance, your grades or whatever can be traced to the absence of unconditional love. Go to your source when you are experiencing fear and you will find fears dissipating almost instantly.

⊙ Remember that love is experienced in your thoughts and in your acts of oneness. The more you consider yourself connected to the divine source, the more you will act in loving ways to all others.

⊙ Acquire a private, nonpublicized and regular habit of meditating. With every breath you take, feel yourself taking in unconditional love. With every exhalation, expel thoughts of fear. This personal exercise can be your lifeline to unconditional love and to the world of manifesting.

When you go outside for a walk, use your breath to bring in the essence of love and feel it flowing throughout your body. Simply use your breath as a means of inhaling love from the divine source, and exhaling fear in the next breath. You will feel yourself relaxing and knowing more joy and freedom.

☉ Pick one day to practice this exercise with a partner of your choice. Make a decision to think, act and radiate nothing but unconditional love for the entire twenty-four-hour period, including your dreams. Every moment of this mutually agreed upon day will be infused with only love.

This means that the moment a moralizing or judgmental thought enters, you immediately shift it out of your inner field and replace it with one of unconditional love. If this works for you for one day, see if you can extend it for another day or two. The longer you can stay with this exercise, the more dramatic the changes.

You will begin to notice synchronistic events showing up and you will feel as if God is taking special care of you. You will notice an increase in energy; an interesting shift in your dreams as they become more intense and spiritual; you will observe yourself attracting things that previously seemed to stay away; you will most assuredly note an increase in joy, bliss and a growth in your relationships as well.

☉ Make a decision to turn over your most difficult challenges in the area of unconditional love to God. Simply turn them over with a request such as, "I have been unable to bring love into my life in these areas, and I am asking for your divine guidance in accomplishing this. I still think angry and hateful thoughts toward these people, and I am asking you to show me the way to unconditional love."

By acknowledging that you feel powerless, you admit that your conditioning and life experiences have not given you the tools to radiate love in these places. But you are also acknowledging that you know there is a higher energy and you ask that higher force to guide you. By turning it over, you place your complete trust in the God force and admit that you cannot break the ego's stronghold.

⊙ In your silent moments of prayer do not be afraid to ask for help. If you want to remove fear and hatred in the spirit of wanting peace, help will be forthcoming. Place no restrictions on how that help is to show up in your life. Simply ask honestly, and when it does show up, give thanks.

⊙ Know the connection between manifesting your heart's desire and unconditional love. Unconditional love is the energy of the universe, it is what God is, and, therefore, what you are as well. Without your connection to this love, you lose your connection to the creative processes.

You cannot attract to yourself that which you are already connected to if you have short-circuited the connection. The presence of unconditional love is in all things that you wish to attract as well as in you. Keep it honestly, and you keep your ability to "know that ye are a god." Lose it, and you lose your godliness. It is that simple.

Remind yourself of this when you ask why your desires aren't showing up in your life. The answer will invariably have something to do with an absence of unconditional love someplace in your inner world.

○ You do not need to fool yourself with unconditional love. If you do not love the personality of another, be open and honest about it, but you can still love the essence, the truth of everyone on this planet and beyond. See the unfolding in everyone, even if their behavior conflicts with what you know to be divine and holy. Know that their egos have gotten a stranglehold on them and twisted their divine essence right out of their behavior, but still send love to the essence that is behind that action.

The more you are able to see past the personality and the individual behavior, the more you will be a beacon of light for the entire planet. It is through a change in consciousness that our world is going to be transformed, and that new consciousness is one in which love is going to triumph over the passions of the ego. Send love out past the appearance with which you are in disagreement and it may shift right before your eyes.

○ Make your word law! Keep this harmony within yourself and you will experience love in virtually all settings. If you say it, live up to it lovingly. This gives you a sense of inner balance that is missing in those who live with self-repudiation and guilt. The more you practice "My word is law. I must keep it," the more balanced your life becomes.

The universe runs on balance, and the energy that keeps it in balance is love. By declaring yourself as a person who keeps his word, you align yourself with the loving essence of the world.

I have witnessed unconditional love in action in the story of Kaye O'Bara, who has been caring for her comatose daughter for twenty-seven years. On an hourly basis—I (along with my wife Marcelene) told her story in a short inspirational book titled *A Promise Is a Promise* and I urge you to familiarize youself with this truly astonishing saga of unconditional love in action—you will feel the inspiration as you read this remarkable story and you will know that you will be helping them out as well, since all royalties go directly to these two divine souls.

This concludes the sixth principle for manifesting. Unconditional love is the cornerstone of your mental picturing. You refuse to allow any contrary, ego-driven thought to enter the inner kingdom of love.

If you activate this principle you will have revealed a truth that eludes most people. It is with unconditional love that you find your true connection to the divine energy that is in all things. It is a choice you can make. You were given the choice to express your free will. It is your gift from God.

When you express love, you align with that same love that was granted to you with the gift of your free will. When you express anger, hatred, envy and violence, you have allied yourself with the ego, and have prevented yourself from truly being a co-creator of your life with the divine source of energy that we call God.

MEDITATING TO THE SOUND OF CREATION

———————— ☉ ☉ ☉ *The Seventh Principle*

T his seventh principle of manifesting will challenge your conditioning more than any of the other eight principles. However, while it contradicts your beliefs about how you fit into the universe, it also expands your ability to create and attract the objects of your heart's desire. This principle describes a very practical application of manifesting at the same time that it invites you to open up to a new idea and a very different practice each day.

I can assure you that there is much to learn and gain from this practice of sound meditation. I have been using it with wondrous results. Others who have done this meditation on a regular basis have experienced dramatic shifts in their lives, and have been able to manifest what they previously believed to be impossible.

As you begin opening yourself to this soul-nourishing practice of chanting to the sounds of creation, spend some time carefully rereading the other eight principles. When you begin to practice these two daily manifestation meditations, you need to trust in your highest self and meditate with unconditional love. Reviewing the other eight principles will help to make trust and love available.

I carefully studied a great deal of spiritual literature before writing this seventh principle. Using sounds to change the vibrations of our frequency is a spiritual practice that has remained obscure over the centuries. Many of the ancient masters kept these secrets of manifesting hidden because of the fear of misuse. In this time of spiritual revolution, individual and collective receptivity is causing these spiritual practices to reappear and reveal their value to us. Meditating with sound can work dramatically in your personal life and can also facilitate a new awareness of our collective abilities to manifest a world free of the demands and petty issues of the ego.

I feel blessed to have a spiritual teacher, Shri Guruji, make these meditations available to me to teach to others who are open to these ideas. I have written about them as I have come to know them, and I present this seventh principle knowing that many of my readers will find it contradictory to their conditioned life experiences. Nevertheless, I know it to be valid and I encourage you to open your mind to your unique capacity to become a manifester for yourself, and more particularly, for the entire planet's evolutionary spiraling upward out of the grip of the ego, which emphasizes separating ourselves from the very force of creation.

This seventh principle is about using sound as a tool for opening to the potential and power of your creative force. Sounds have the power to generate your ability to attract to yourself that which you desire. Three key words describing this principle are the title of the following section.

SOUNDS HAVE POWER

Sounds are a powerful energy. Every sound is a vibration made of waves oscillating at a particular frequency. The frequency range of the human ear is approximately sixteen thousand vibrations, up to roughly forty thousand vibrations, per second. Higher up on the scale, with increasingly faster vibrations, is electricity, at about one thousand million vibrations per second. At two hundred billion vibrations per second we find heat. Light and color are at five hundred billion vibrations per second, and an X ray manifests at two trillion vibrations per second. It is theorized that thoughts and the unknown etheric and spiritual dimensions are in the realm of increased vibrations beyond anything that is calculable at this point in time. Vibrational frequencies are very clearly the very nature of our material universe.

Sound as we hear it is low on the scale, just above

forms, or solids, in its speed of frequency. Sound is the intermediary between the abstract idea and the concrete form of the material world. Sounds literally mold the abstract world of thought and spirit into shapes. "Let there be light, and there was light" is the biblical description of creation. Or in other words "Let the vibrations of light emanate from my command."

In ancient ceremonial rites, words, sounds and shapes combine to achieve certain ends. Each letter in a word signifies a sound and records the expression of a particular sound. Differing sounds were written out for their own purposes.

Sounds have an impact on us in myriad ways. An eidophone is an instrument constructed of a tightly stretched drum surface upon which a pasty substance is spread. Sounds and words are then uttered below the surface, and different sounds produce different shapes and forms in the paste. Some of these are replicas of animals, flowers and other creations of nature. When sand is used rather than paste, the sand forms geometric shapes and designs that correspond to the letters of the alphabet. When the sounds are strident and unpleasant, they produce displeasing patterns. Experiments of this nature illustrate the impact that sounds can have on us.

The discordant and harassing sounds of machines, such as thudding, screaming and grating noises bombarding our consciousness, make it difficult to be serene and peaceful. Discordant sounds can cause internal illness. But sound has healing properties when it is harmonious and soothing. Healing takes place to the accompaniment of soothing harmonies and nature's music interspersed with spiritually nourishing silence.

In addition to healing, sound is used in the creation process, which is the central concern of this seventh principle of spiritual manifestation. When we use the sounds of nature that are most consistent with the act of creation, we begin to attract the material form that we desire from those much higher frequencies that our senses cannot process.

Keep in mind that sound is the vibrational frequency between the world of solid matter or form as we know it and the higher vibrational frequencies of the formless world of universal spirit. Learning how to use sound is a way of harnessing its power for manifesting thought into the world of form. Manifesting is knowing how to make contact with that spiritual vibrational frequency while we are living inside a body in a materialized world.

Sound is the only vibrational frequency that we can utilize and change with our senses. All other frequencies are beyond our ability to harness and experience to change our vibrational frequency. Pay attention to words and sounds because they can attract positive or negative influences into your life. Harmonious sounds are the ones that most contribute to a balanced and creative life.

But before going into the actual use of meditation sounds it is necessary to learn how to prepare yourself to use sounds in your daily meditation. Manifesting is not done by the mind. You need to gain access to a method that will take you beyond the mind to a state of consciousness that transcends your thoughts. This higher state of consciousness beyond the mind is called *siddhi* awareness.

UNDERSTANDING *SIDDHI* CONSCIOUSNESS

Siddhi consciousness is a perfect state of awareness in which there is a complete absence of doubt and no delay between the origination of a thought and its materialization into the world of form. It is an unlimited state of being in which creation occurs instantly, without any time lag from thought to form. When we contemplate this state of grace, our minds immediately begin to challenge this idea and provide us with many reasons as to why it is impossible.

Siddhi consciousness, however, has absolutely nothing to do with the mind. Let that sink in. *Siddhi* consciousness is beyond the mind. This state of graceful being has nothing to do with the mind, whose nature is a constant inner monologue. The mind frets continually about an unlimited number of desires that can never be adequately fulfilled. You can give your body great pleasures with booze and sex; give it fancy automobiles and delectable gourmet meals; body massages and every other imaginable delight. The next morning, when it recovers, your mind has a new list of demands taped to your forehead, asking for more and more of what it can never get enough of. This is the nature of the mind, which is ruled by the ego.

Your mind, then, is only a barrier to experiencing *siddhi* consciousness wherein you are in a state of bliss and complete acceptance and your desires are the same as your experience of life. Your mind blocks the vision of your highest awareness. Deep within you is the awareness of the perfect state, in which your ability to attract to yourself the object of your desires is more immediate and less left to chance than when your mind is in charge. With *siddhi* consciousness you are at peace and your inner knowing begins to replace your thoughts.

Using sound at the level of *siddhi* consciousness is like using a different language. Your highest self has its own language. When your body is stilled and totally in the present, thoughts disappear. Then you can start the exquisite process of meditating with sound. It is the magic of this sound meditation that I am going to explain in the seventh principle. This is a technique to take you beyond the constraints of the ego and the mind, to a place within yourself where you can change your vibrational frequency through the use of the sounds of creation.

The act of creation itself is a sound. When understood and put to use, sound will heighten your awareness of the *siddhi* consciousness within you.

THE MAGIC OF THE SOUNDS OF CREATION

As you begin to incorporate these ideas of the power of sound into your consciousness, going beyond the darkness of your mind to the light of your highest

self, think about these words that open the book of
John in the New Testament: "In the beginning was the
Word, and the Word was with God, and the Word was
God."

The word "God" has the same sound that is in virtually all of the names for the original creator. All recorded
history of humankind, including primitive cultures,
Eastern and Western religions and other traditions,
describes a creator of the word and humankind. Here is
a list of names used for the creator. Can you identify the
sound that is consistent in all of these names?

Ra	Tat
Krishna	Sugmad
Rama	Gaiana
Buddha	Mahanta
Waaken Tanka	Mahavira
Ahdonay	Anu
Brahma	Khoda
Siddha	Akua
Ahura Mazda	Atva
Shiva	Nanak
Jehovah	Osenbula
Maheo	Yahweh
Kami Sama	God
Nagual	Ato
Kali Durga	Allah

The obvious sound that is in all of these names for
the creator is the sound *aaah*. This sound is the sound
of creation, and it is the sound of joy. *Aaah* expresses a

feeling of bliss and joy. The sounds of creation and joy are synonymous.

It is not an accident that the name for the creator in all languages contains the sound *aaah*. The sound *aaah* is the only sound that humans make effortlessly by simply taking in a breath, and without moving the lips, tongue, jaw or teeth, letting the sound of *aaah* flow out. If you move any of these, the sound changes. *Aaah* is the sound of effortless perfection, as is creation itself effortless and perfect.

This sound of *aaah*, the sound of creation, is one that you will want to use as you practice the language of *siddhi* consciousness. The sound takes you beyond the incessant self-dialogue that characterizes your mind. When you repeat the sound of *aaah* in connection with your manifestation meditation practice, you are literally repeating the name of God.

In *Reflection of the Self,* Swami Muktananda gives these words to his devotees who desire to know more about the state of *siddhi* consciousness.

> With eyes brimming with love, sing His name.
> All inner mysteries will be disclosed.
> Every bird and plant
> will reveal itself to you as Brahman.
> The knowledge of Vedanta will manifest everywhere.
> O dear one, keep chanting God's name
> while sitting, or standing,
> or involved in the world.
> Never forget Him.
> Unite your mind with the Self.

He explained that these names for God have specific combinations of inherently powerful syllables that have the ability to call forth the experience of God within us. Ancient sages vocalized the sounds vibrating in the different chakras of the body during meditation. Making these sounds acquaints us, perhaps for the first time, with the subtle God force within ourselves.

Over two thousand years ago, Patanjali set down his highly celebrated yoga sutras, which were designed to guide seekers to the highest state of awareness, known as *siddhi* consciousness. Patanjali is considered, by millions of people who have studied his yoga sutras, to be the greatest scientist of the inner world to have ever lived.

Patanjali offered this advice to students seeking the power of the highest state of consciousness: "Repeat and meditate on *Aum*." *Aum* is a symbol for the universal sound of creation. Patanjali explained that when the body is left, the mind disappears and what is heard is the sound of *aum*. Repeating this sound causes the disappearance of obstacles and an awakening of a new higher consciousness that is the creative energy. When we practice we actually become the universal sound itself. It is the yoga (the coming together) of the observer and the observed.

Continually chant God's name is the advice of the masters of self-awareness to those who seek to participate in the act of creating and manifesting. The sound of *aaah* is the sound of God. Repeat it several times and you will immediately feel the sense of joy and nourishment that occurs. Make the repetition of the name of God a daily meditation practice and you will literally transform yourself into this universal sound of creation. You will become one with the sound that mediates between the world of form and the highest frequencies of the spiritual world.

The *aaah* sound meditation will benefit from your developing a mental picture of your own creation capacities for manifesting. One way to accomplish this is to see yourself as a generator projecting energy vibrating with the *aaah* God sound. Picture the sound emanating through chakra openings in your body, connecting with what you want to attract or create in your world of form.

THE CREATION MEDITATION AND THE TWO MANIFESTING CHAKRAS

Of the total of the seven chakras of the body there are two that are significant in learning this manifesting technique. The base chakra, or the sex center, is one, and the third eye chakra, or the mind chakra, located between the eyebrows, is the other. Imagine a channel that exists in your body between the base chakra and your third eye. You are going to clear this imaginary passageway between these two chakras and feel yourself open the third eye so that you can imaginatively project your manifesting energy out of the new opening.

The base chakra is the center of procreation. The third eye chakra is the chakra for the purpose of manifestation. Think of your third eye, which is invisible to the naked eye, as the part of you that makes extended contact with the physical world. This third eye chakra can voluntarily register or see the vibrations of dimensions beyond the physical plane, but only when you can convince yourself of this truth and can unclog this opening. You are attempting to open this third eye through the language of your *siddhi* consciousness, using your rational left brain, which maintains that this is nonsense, and impossible as well.

Now remembering that the sound of *aaah* is the sound of joy as well as the God sound ("and the Word was God in the beginning"), think about the sound that accompanies the process of procreation. The sound of *aaah* is the most common sound heard in the very act of procreation, and more often than not, God's name is repeated as a soul arrives from the world of the unseen into the world of materialized form: "Oh God!" "Oh my God!" "Aaah!"

Initially this may seem amusing, yet it is valid and incontrovertible that these are universal clues to the process of manifestation. The energy released through the root or base chakra brings about procreation. And what has taken place? A release of energy from the base chakra received by another base chakra, and a soul connects to form from the unseen to the manifested, all accompanied by the sound of *aaah*. There is no doubt about this one. The energy released through the third eye chakra is called re-creation, or manifestation.

Learning this technique of sound manifesting involves really nothing more than opening up the channel that exists between these two chakras in your body. By repeating the sound *aaah* in the manner I have described at the end of this seventh principle, and feeling that energy moving up from the procreation center of your being to the third eye, and then ultimately opening that third eye with your own etheric energy by using this sound, you put out into the world an unconditionally loving energy that will bring about the creation of your heart's desire. With manifesting, you send out a release of energy from the "mind chakra," or third eye, and connect it to that which you desire.

As Muktananda repeatedly reminded his followers, "Catching a glimpse of the beauty of reality is a gift made possible through *Shaktipat* (divine energy that is transferred directly) and through the power of repeating God's name, whether through chanting, prayer, or mantra repetition." And with steadfast practice, as the great teachers tell us, we will be free of everything that keeps us from living constantly in the awareness that "all this is God, all this is God." (*Darshan Magazine,* September 1994, p. 3.)

Opening the third eye is an inner exercise of putting your attention at the third eye, or mind chakra, and projecting through it, feeling the joy that is associated with the sound. You experience it leaving the limits of your physical body and embracing that which you want to manifest and bringing it back to you. It is tuning into the vibration of creation by leaving the constraints of your body/mind and opening up the channel between your procreation center and your manifestation center. With this passageway cleared of obstacles, you are immersed in the grace of soul-nourishing bliss with the daily repetition of the *aaah* meditation.

Implement this sound meditation in your morning practice. You will be harmonizing with a sound of peace and joy, as well as participating in the idea that you and God are one in the universal sense. The sound brings you to that awareness since it is not a word that the mind can then take and distort into an ego-dominated blueprint. It is a sound that transcends the rational workings of the mind.

I have created a cassette tape and a compact disc called *Meditations for Manifesting,* which guides you through this morning meditation using my voice to help you stay focused on the sound. In addition, this recording guides you through the second meditation, which takes place in the evening and also places the emphasis on the third eye chakra. However, the emphasis of the evening meditation for manifesting is different. Here you put your attention on gratitude for all that has manifested into your life. This is also the subject matter of the ninth and final principle.

THE SOUND OF THAT WHICH IS MANIFESTED

There is a second sound that reflects the vibrational frequency of manifestations in the physical plane. This sound is *om.* If you reduced anything that you can observe on the physical plane to its ultimate sound vibration, you would hear the sound of *om.* This is the sound that women of ancient times meditated to while bringing their babies into the world. Whereas *aaah* is the sound of creation, *om* is the sound of that which is already created. *Om* expresses gratitude for all that has manifested.

There is a basic relationship between our level of awareness and the vibrations of the universe. Being aware of this makes it possible to tune these vibrations to the state of mind that you desire. This is why I include the *om* meditation in the manifestation process. Repeating the *om* sound in the evening tunes you to a higher state of awareness and to gratitude for all that has manifested into your life. You will then be in sync with your immediate surroundings.

Repeating this sound as a mantra of gratitude is one of the most joyous feelings you will ever experience, causing you to be in harmony with your environment rather than in opposition to it in any way. You will feel strongly connected to your life rather than experiencing the ego-based feeling of controlling your environment.

Using the *om* sound is a way of bonding to all that manifests for you, in whatever form it shows up. It creates a peaceful space and contributes to your identifying with the manifesting principle. You feel as if you and God are finally on the same team rather than in a boss-employee relationship. Your ability to do this *om* meditation regularly will help you to value what you are manifesting, and to feel spiritually connected.

The sound of *om* while meditating is also centered at the third eye chakra. Project the energy of thanksgiving from this chakra and you will feel an opening at the third eye. Then extend your etheric energy vibrating to the sound of all that is in the physical world through the imaginary opening in the area of the third eye. As you make this sound and become familiar with it, you will coalesce with the joy that is associated with it. You will feel lighter, more refreshed and more connected to all that is in your world and all that has manifested for you. On the tape and compact disc I have included affirmations of gratitude that I repeat while you are meditating.

At this point I hope you are aware of the importance of, and the need for, using the *om* meditation in the evening and the *aaah* manifesting meditation in the morning. These two sounds, used on a daily basis, preferably in the morning and the evening, form the basis for your becoming adept at connecting with what you desire, and understanding totally the message of this book, which is that you indeed manifest your own desires and destiny.

I would not even consider sitting down to write without first sitting in quiet meditation for twenty to thirty minutes of doing the *aaah* meditation. It is in this space that I gather the energy of creation by repeating continuously the *aaah* sound of joyous creation. Then, in the evening, when I have completed my writing for the day, I do the meditation of gratitude, employing the *om* sound, which is the sound of all that I have created on my typewriter that day.

This simple ritual puts me in a state of grace, and provides me with an inner knowing that I am in relationship with the creative God force of the universe, and that I am exceedingly grateful for such a divine relationship. It is what I call the sacred relationship.

Without it I would be unable to manifest this or any other book.

Once you understand these two sounds, and you know the power of these vibrations, you will want to put this awareness into practice. You will find a detailed account of precisely how to do these manifesting meditations on a daily basis in the next section.

THE PRACTICE OF MEDITATING FOR MANIFESTING

Manifesting and meditating cannot be separated. They are like the crest and the trough of the wave, separate and distinct from each other, but always together. You cannot become adept at manifesting the desires of your heart if you are unwilling to devote time to the practice of meditation.

Meditation is simply the act of being quiet with yourself and shutting down the constant monologue that fills the inner space of your being. It is stopping the constant bombardment of thoughts and the seemingly endless chatter filling your inner world. That inner noise is a shield preventing you from knowing the highest self.

Engaging in sound meditation is a useful way of accomplishing inner silence and removing the influences of the constant chatter that is largely produced by the ego. The attention of the mind is diverted from the millions of scattered thoughts and is brought back to the awareness of the sound itself. The sound serves as a mantra, keeping you centered and silencing the chatter.

The best times for meditating using this manifesting technique of repetitive sounds are at sunrise and sunset. If you are unaccustomed to arising at or before sunrise, make an effort to establish this discipline for a trial period of ninety days. If this is impossible, then use whatever your time of awakening is for the *aaah* meditation. However, I would encourage you to challenge any preset, conditioned belief you may have concerning your ability to get up before sunrise for the manifesting meditation. Your beliefs about requiring a certain number of hours of sleep, or not being able to get out of bed, or treasuring sleep more than anything and similar reasons are the result of your conditioning and often represent nothing more than excuses.

What you want to do is to establish yourself as a disciplined person. Early morning, particularly prior to sunrise, is the best time of day to awaken. The silence allows you to feel close to God. It is the time when your mind and heart are the clearest and least distracted. You can feel the energy of healing and solutions in the silence of the early morning, particularly between the hours of three and six A.M. Use specific acts of personal courage to awaken during these hours, knowing that the time spent in a manifesting meditation will provide you with far more rest than the remaining hours of your scheduled sleep.

The sun is a gigantic source of energy for our planet and everything that grows on it. When the sun first begins to show itself in the morning, the energy of the sun breaking out of the darkness is most intense. This is the ideal time to begin your manifesting meditation. I recommend that you find a comfortable place to sit, without regard for a particular posture or position. What makes you feel most relaxed and at peace is the perfect posture. If at all possible, it is advisable to do this outdoors; however, this is by no means a requirement. Gently place your forefinger and thumb together on each hand. Close your eyes and allow yourself approximately twenty minutes for this morning practice.

Take in a few long, deep breaths and exhale, becoming aware of the pattern of your breathing and the feeling of filling your lungs. Then place your attention on the root or base chakra (the sex center) and move your attention up the passageway between your root chakra and your third eye chakra. Think of this as a channel that has been clogged, and think of the third eye space as an opening that has been sealed for a long time that you are going to open with your inner etheric energy. Now take a deeper, longer, breath of air, filling your lungs, and as you release the breath say out loud the sound of *aaah* with as much emotion and volume as you can manage.

Place your attention on clearing the channel with this sound of *aaah*. While you are doing the *aaah* meditation, add to your mental picture what it is that you would like to be able to create or manifest, without being at all attached to how it will surface in your life. (I have explained in detail in the eighth principle the importance of not making demands on the how.) What you are doing is focusing on the feeling that you will have as this desire manifests in the concrete world of your life.

While you meditate for approximately twenty minutes in the beginning of your day, repeat the sound of *aaah* as your mantra for the entire time. However, only do it out loud and with emotion for approximately the first one third of the time. Move your attention up and down the inner passageway between the root chakra and the third eye chakra using the sound of *aaah*. Then remain focused on the third eye chakra. You are now going to open up the third eye.

With the inner energy that you are feeling from the sound of creation resonating within you, open the third eye in your mental picture, and propel the creative force through it into the world of form. Imagine its release from your inner being to a point at which it circles the world and surrounds the objects of your desire. Trust that this energy will connect with the universal energy that is the God force and will send the object of your desire into your immediate world. This must be done in accordance with all nine of the principles of manifesting that are explained in this book, which means you have an absence of doubt, complete trust, unconditional love and a knowing that this power of attraction is within you and in all things.

Gradually you will begin to experience an overwhelming sense of bliss and peace in the sound of creation. Then you will feel the need to lower the volume. For the next approximately one third of the morning meditation say the *aaah* sound softer and softer. Stay focused on the third eye, which is now open and sending out this creation energy, and the feeling of your desire manifesting. If you feel distracted or your attention shifts, return to the third eye and the feeling of your manifestation materializing for you. Remember, you are not demanding anything, you are not telling God how to do this work, you are experiencing in the third eye the strong feeling of knowing and the bliss of this sound repeated in a quieter and quieter fashion.

For the final one third of your morning meditation, repeat the sound of *aaah* to yourself silently as a mantra, and keep your attention on the third eye and the glorious feeling of gratitude that you are already experiencing for having this manifest, however it will, into your life. When you have completed approximately twenty to thirty minutes of this manifesting meditation, your morning session will be complete.

The objects of your desire can be unlimited, and they can run the full gamut of human potentiality. Some people have used this meditation to manifest peace for themselves or those they love, to center themselves on a healing, or to bring a relationship into their life. Others have used it for such matters as selling a house, getting a promotion, overcoming an addiction, attracting money or whatever. The possibilities are unlimited. I have received hundreds of letters from people describing the success they have had with this meditation when they practice it, using all nine of these principles with integrity.

If you have read this far into this book, you are demonstrating your interest in learning to become a spiritual manifester. If you know that the power to manifest is within you, then do this ancient practice of repeating the name of God in an almost chantlike ritual each and every morning, with your attention on the feeling and the third eye. What you are really doing when you do this morning *aaah* meditation is resonating with the words "In the beginning was the word, and the word was God." The act of manifesting is the beginning of something being created in your life. The word *is* God, which is to say, the *aaah* sound is the sound of God.

The evening meditation is best practiced at sunset if possible. Once again, as the sun sinks below the horizon there is a coronalike expression of energy that is greatest just as the sun leaves the horizon and for a few moments immediately after the sun disappears from our vision. Now you practice the sound of *om*, which is the meditation of gratitude. I have detailed this principle of gratitude in the ninth and final principle explained in this book.

Briefly, the practice is identical to the morning meditation, with the exception that you are not now asking to manifest anything. Instead, at the end of your daylight, or as you retire, you are simply saying thank you to the universal intelligence that we call God for all that has manifested in your life. Take in deep breaths just as you did in the morning, clear the channel between your base chakra and your third eye chakra, and mentally picture all that you have received and project that energy out forcefully through the opening of the third eye. You are expelling into the universe beyond your immediate body an energy of gratitude, using the affirmations that I have included in the ninth principle, and which I say aloud during the guided meditation on the cassette and compact disc titled *Meditations for Manifesting*.

The sound of *om* is said aloud for the first third of your meditation, then gradually more quietly, and ultimately silently, always focusing grateful attention on the third eye and feeling that energy going back to the universal source of energy that we call God. The sound of *om* is the sound of the material world. It is the sound that makes us feel most at home here in the material world since it is the essential sound of all experience in this phenomenal world. When you repeat this sound, you are in harmony with your environment.

The final part of this meditation is the last sound you hear before you go to sleep each night. The very first sound you hear in the morning is generally one of *aaah*. It is the sound that you make when you yawn or stretch. Be aware of this first sound and be willing to acknowledge it as your own vibrational frequency of the new day that you are manifesting. However, the final sound you hear within yourself before going to sleep can be a combination of these two sounds of *aaah* and *om*.

You may recall that I defined enlightenment earlier in this book as the ability to be immersed in and surrounded by peace. "Peace" is the key word here. It is not an accident that the sounds of *aaah* and *om*, when combined, translate to the word that means peace or enlightenment, *Shalom. Shaaah . . . looom*. The sound of that which you wish to manifest, and that which is already manifested, equate to peace. By saying these two sounds to yourself as you drift off to sleep, you are beginning the act of enlightened *siddhi* consciousness. You are becoming at one with all that is peaceful and all that provides for us. It is also not an accident that the primary sound of spiritual joy is the sound of *aaah* in hallelujah, and it is the sound found in the word that ends every prayer, "amen."

This concludes the meditation practice of learning to vibrate to the sound of creating and creation. It is a part of the ancient wisdom that is being practiced and revealed more and more as we move into the spiritual revolution. Give this glorious, peaceful, enlightening manifestation meditation practice a three-month trial period in your life, using each of the nine principles outlined in this book, and see if you do not experience your heart's desire appearing without your putting any demands or rules on the universal God force. The willingness to allow it to manifest as it will, permitting creation to reveal itself by and by, is the subject of the eighth principle of manifesting. Hallelujah. *Shalom.*

PATIENTLY DETACH FROM THE OUTCOME

—————————— ☉ ☉ ☉ *The Eighth Principle*

*I*n the seventh principle, on the use of the sound meditation, I emphasized the importance of placing your attention not on the outcome and how it will show up in your life, but on the feelings that you are experiencing as you picture your desire manifesting. The eighth principle of spiritual manifesting has at its heart the experience of that feeling. The manner of how and when what is desired shows up is something that you must not try to control.

During the time I have taught this meditation I have often been asked questions like this one: "If I do this meditation as you suggest, can I really win the lottery?" My response to this question is, "How would you feel if you won the lottery?" The answers are something similar to "I would feel blessed, secure, ecstatic, content." It is this feeling picture that is crucial for one to have in order to activate the eighth principle. It is an illusion that you must have some *thing* like a winning lottery ticket in order to feel blessed, secure, ecstatic or content.

Manifesting is not about making demands of God and the universe. Manifesting is a cooperative venture in which your intention is aligned with divine intelligence. That intelligence is in all things and in you simultaneously. You are not separate from that which you would like to manifest. It is you, you are it. There is only one power in the universe, and you are connected to that power. Demanding that God send your desire according to your timetable and design reinforces the incorrect idea of God as a separate energy.

Imagining an intelligence in the universe that is devoid of individual personality is a way of beginning to understand this eighth principle. This unusual and perhaps difficult concept will help to make the eighth principle more manageable.

INTELLIGENCE APART FROM INDIVIDUALITY

Most of us believe that the recognition of any other individual affirms a point at which our own individuality ceases and the other's begins. This belief is part of our conditioning, and it imposes a great deal of limitation on us. Early on we learned that "I am not that other because I am myself."

If this pattern were ascribed to the universal mind it would describe a God that at some point ceased and something else began. The description of universal would not apply because the God energy would not include all things. To be universal and to recognize anything as being outside itself would be to deny its very being. So, the nature of universal intelligence is an absence of individual personality.

The all-pervading spirit is an impersonal life force that gives rise to all that is manifested. The universal spirit permeates all space and all that is manifested and we all are a part of that. You are in an impersonal and intensely intelligent ocean of life that is all around, under and in everything, including you. Though you have been conditioned to believe that you are individual, you are actually a part of the grand universal nature that is infinite in its possibilities.

This undifferentiated intelligence responds to you when you recognize it. If you believe that the world runs by chance, or by your personal demands, then universal mind will present you with a hodgepodge of reactions without any recognizable order. However, when you cease believing that you are a separate personality with individual intelligence, you begin to have a new clarity.

From the perspective of an intelligence that is universal and undifferentiated, ask yourself what the relationship of this universal mind is to you. It cannot have "favorites" if it is the root and support for everything and everyone. Lacking individuality, it cannot be in conflict with your desires. Being universal, it cannot be simply shut off from you.

All these statements characterize this all-producing mind as responsive to you when you understand your relationship to it. This universal, all-pervading principle has nature in common with you. When you solve this riddle of the ego, you have a new wisdom regarding your ability to apply this eighth principle of manifestation.

You cannot exhaust the infinite, so your possession of it means that you have the ability to differentiate it as you desire. Your task is to bring the universal within your grasp by raising yourself to the level of that which is universal rather than bringing the universal down to a level of misperceived individuality that is separate from the universal. You need only to recognize it to attract it to yourself rather than asking it to recognize you and bring you to it. Having learned a different set of principles, all of this may sound a bit confusing. Yet it is crucially important for you to know this before moving along on the path of manifesting.

Recognize the universal as a part of all that you are, and that all that you are is undifferentiated from all that is. Keep repeating this new awareness. Then know that if you fail to recognize the universal as undifferentiated, it will present itself to you in exactly that fashion, as a mishmash of energy that you cannot grasp, as chaos rather than a cosmos, and as a system in which you are separated from all that you desire.

So, remove any and all demands from your desires, and shift to the inner, knowing that you are bringing the universal intelligence into your life, and that you will leave the how and when up to that intelligence, without judging, demanding or insisting upon your own personality's prerequisites. Your knowing is enough. Then, cultivate the power of patient detachment from the outcome.

THE POWER OF INFINITE PATIENCE

This provocative line is from *A Course in Miracles:* "Those who are certain of the outcome can afford to wait, and without anxiety." This is the mainstay of infinite patience. The notion of certainty and patience go together. When you trust and know that you are connected to that universal, all-providing intelligence, then you simply allow yourself the virtue of patience. You place no time constraints on your manifestation and you go about the affairs of your life with an inner awareness that says, "I've got all the time that I need, and I am certain of the outcome, so I will allow it to show up as it will, in due time."

The secret to being patient is in the certainty of the outcome. When that certainty is manifested in you in the form of trust and a knowing, you can then turn your thoughts away from the desired outcome. Without anger or anxiety, you are able to turn your attention to whatever it is that occupies your daily life schedule.

Your knowing and your infinite patience put you at ease. You have practiced all of the principles of spiritual manifestation, and then you have allowed the universe to handle the details. Your inner sense is that what you want to manifest is already here, and your inner attention is on the feeling of well-being that you are already blessed with what it is you seek. Consequently, there is no pressure for you to make it show up immediately.

This inner bliss is a function of the power of your infinite patience. Later on in *A Course in Miracles* we are reminded that "Patience is natural to the teacher of God. All he sees is certain outcome, at a time perhaps unknown to him as yet, but not in doubt." I love this idea of having a certainty about the outcome and being unconcerned about the details.

When we become impatient, we literally devalue ourselves and our connection to the divine Holy Spirit. Impatience is a failure to trust in the universal intelligence, and it implies that we are separate from the all-providing spirit. Impatience implies that our ego is the boss of desire. This form of self-importance needs to be addressed.

When you are certain about the outcome, and unconcerned with the how and when, you have cultivated the power of infinite patience, and simultaneously you have detached yourself from the outcome. When this detachment takes place, you are able to go about your daily business of raising your children, doing your work or training, meditating and communing with God and just patiently observing. Patience is natural when you trust in the oneness of the universal intelligence.

One of the ways to develop patience is to contemplate how patient God has been with you. When you were in times of denial, or self-abuse, or self-absorption, or hatred, God was infinitely patient. God does not scold or punish you when you are off the sacred path, nor does God desert you. This is the same kind of patience that you want to develop.

Infinite patience is a sign of trust, and it calls upon infinite love to produce results in your life. When you let go of impatience, you are aligned with the God force, and all of the anxiety that tells you what is lacking and missing in your life is gone. Anxiety produces fear and self-pity and attaches you to time. When fear-based impatience takes over, you lose your infinite self and become once again subject to the ego, which has no patience with anything about infinitude.

The ego wants what it wants, and it wants it now. If it is not satisfied, it will convince you of what a rotten place this is and how you cannot trust anything but your differentiated self, even though that self has produced the feelings of lack all along. If you do satisfy the ego, a new list of demands will appear the next day. The anxiety level will increase as you complete these new demands. This continues as long as the ego is in charge of your life.

But when you recognize the connection between your infinite self and the God force, you will know that God has been patient with you no matter how long it took you to come around, regardless of how far you may have wandered and no matter how much you may have refused to listen.

Infinite patience produces almost immediate results in your life. You become free when you relax your insistence to have it now, and you increase your awareness that you actually do have it now, already, even though it may not have shown up as you would like it in your immediate surroundings. As an infinitely patient person you know that you are already where you want to be, that there are no accidents and that all that appears to be missing is nothing more than an illusion perpetrated by your ego.

With this awareness, impatience leaves, and you stop looking for results of your manifestation meditation. You turn your thoughts to the affairs of your life, knowing that you are not alone. Your patience allows you to remain in silent appreciation for all that is manifested in your life. This practice of patient detachment from outcome is a foreign concept to those of us who have been taught that goals, success symbols and the accumulation of merit badges are the ways to feel important and fit into our culture. You have achieved peace with your infinite patience, and peace is what enlightenment is all about.

What follows is a guide for living with the seeming paradox of attempting to manifest something into your life, and at the same time not being attached to when and how it shows up.

A STEP-BY-STEP PLAN FOR PUTTING PATIENT DETACHMENT INTO YOUR MANIFESTATION PRACTICE

⊙ Understand the essence of what you desire. What you desire is not necessarily in the realm of *things*. If you want to manifest money, for example, notice if your attention is centered on the dollars or on the experience and feeling of financial security. Ask yourself what you want this money for. Put your attention on the joyous experiences that you associate with what you are desiring rather than focusing on a new automobile or a new boss or a different partner. The experience is the essence of your desire.

The essence is always located where you experience your feelings. By putting your attention on the inner feelings, you shift from being gratified by externals to the experience of gratification. The essence of your desire is a feeling of well-being and joy and an alignment with the universal spirit. Then you will see many things showing up in your life that will lead you to the inner-directed path. They may have nothing to do with what you originally thought you wanted or needed.

You may feel that you truly want to manifest more income and a promotion, but if you find the essence of this desire, it may revolve around more security and a sense of well-being. Detach yourself from the in-the-world promotion and increase in pay. Instead, put your manifesting energy around the very essence of your wanting to feel more secure and less stressed. You will probably begin to see things arriving in your life and reducing your anxiety. Again, they may seem to have very little to do with what you originally thought you wanted.

⊙ Banish the doubt and enter into the realm of certainty. Remove all doubts concerning your ability to manifest the essence of your desires. Review what you have read up until this point and remind yourself, whenever any doubt creeps in, that you and the universal intelligence are one and the same, and that this universal intelligence is in all things. You know this and you know that you can connect to this energy in a way that will fulfill the essence of your desires. I recommend that you review the second principle in this book, and the entire chapter titled "Banish the Doubt" in *Your Sacred Self,* if you want to reinforce this idea.

When you have removed the doubt about your ability to manifest, it will be easy to detach yourself from the outcome and all of the details. Your trust in yourself and in the divine energy of the universe is all that you will need.

⊙ Leave your expectations and go about your business. Once you have put your *aaah* meditation out into the universe through the opening of the third eye, simply forget about it and get on with the business of your daily life. Do not keep looking for reasons to disbelieve your ability to attract to yourself what you desire.

Practice the patience that God has always displayed toward you during your tumultuous times. You will find comfort in the silent inner knowing and in your relationship to God.

Maintain your daily work and play regime with

a new sense of peace, originating in your inner knowing about what is manifesting for you. Remain completely detached from the inclination to measure and calculate what is and is not showing up for you.

In fact, it may take some time after your desires have manifested for you to even be aware that they are here! There may be a time when you notice that it has already begun to happen and you realize that you did not see it right away because you had let go and let God handle it for you. This is an indication that you have been able to master this principle of patient detachment from outcome.

⊙ Maintain privacy about your desires. As was stated earlier, sharing your manifestation efforts decreases the energy and deflects that energy into the ego's need to gain approval. You want the energy of your manifestation to be direct and as pure as possible. Furthermore, you want to avoid dissipating the energy that you are projecting by preventing it from becoming involved with any ego needs.

When you are patiently detached, you have also detached yourself from any need to gain approval for your efforts. Of course, you may wish ultimately to share the results of your spiritual manifesting, but while you are incubating this divine experience with God, make every effort to keep it a private affair. A need to share it at this stage is an indication that you are focused on out-come and are attached to the results.

⊙ Be aware of the cues that your desires are mani-festing. Keep in mind that the way things will show up in your life is not necessarily related to what your rational brain has indicated. Things may begin popping into your life that were never there before, and which may surprise you as you notice them more and more frequently.

You will also begin to notice more of a connec-tion between your thoughts and the object of those thoughts materializing in your life. Things that you used to label coincidences will become more and more evident as you practice these principles of manifesting. You will see people showing up to help you after you have thought about these needed helpers. You will find objects appearing that were in your mind, and which you have forgotten about, but now are showing up more and more.

Someone will mention a particular movie or song or some other apparently irrelevant item, and you will hear it over and over, or the out-of-print movie you had mentioned wanting to see will arrive in your video store that very same day. Be aware of what you have been thinking about in relationship to what you want to manifest. These are cues that will begin to pop up in a multitude of delightful and unexpected ways.

All of these synchronistic events and happenings are the result of beginning to live in a heightened state of awareness. You are consciously making contact with the universal source of all energy that has been below your conscious level before, but is now beginning to appear above the surface. Pay close attention to the cues as they surface, and gently tell yourself, "It's working. I can see the results and I know that they are due to my using these principles and my meditation practices. I'll continue privately to do what I am doing."

⊙ Act immediately on the cues that arrive by acknowledging them. When you acknowledge the early signs of arrival of what you wish to manifest, you are giving your inner energy a positive charge and recognizing the divine universal intelligence. This recognition is essential to the continuation of this manifesting process.

When you see it starting to show up, give silent thanks and say to yourself, "I see the results of my connecting to the universal source. I notice the presence of that particular person who offered to help me, and I know he or she was sent to me by God. I give thanks, and I will make every attempt to use this manifestation for the good of humanity rather than for my own ego gratification."

⊙ Don't think of your manifestation as a special favor. The universal intelligence that we call God is not an individual personality and it will not dispense special favors to you or anyone else. To see manifestation as a favor is to begin the process of bargaining with God and believing in your separateness from all other living beings. The process of manifesting is a spiritual practice in that it is your recognition that you and the divine source of all energy are one and the same.

This oneness has no judgments about anyone being more entitled to abundance than anyone else. It is everywhere and in all things, and it shows up when you, as a localized particle of that divine source, recognize your connection and are open to it working in your life.

While gratitude is such an important part of this consciousness that it represents the ninth and final principle of spiritual manifesting, it is not appreciation for a special favor. The ego thrives on making you special and distinct from others and, therefore, more deserving of its multitude of demands. The ego would love you to think of these manifestations as special favors, because in doing so, you would reinforce your separation from that source.

Your desires manifest because you are in perfect alignment with your source of creation, and because you are not placing any limitations on what can come into your life. Ignore your ego's efforts to make you think that you are receiving God's richest blessings in the form of having your desires materialize because you are special.

Instead, be thankful and use these blessings in the service of others and in deep gratitude for your own spiritual essence. Your identification is no longer exclusively with the physical body, and your infinite soul is recognized as your true essence. It is this recognition that is responsible for your manifestation results, not that you have been singled out. Remember again, the universal intelligence called God cannot possibly be singled out, since it is everywhere in everything.

⊙ View any and all obstacles as lessons, not indications of failure. Keep in mind that you are practicing patience and detachment from outcome. When anything appears to be an obstacle, do not use that material fact to deny the existence of the universal energy that is your essence.

Once again, this is the work of the ego, which wants you to believe that it, rather than God, is in charge. If the ego can convince you that this stuff is all nonsense, and that these obstacles are proof positive that God is ignoring you, then you will be back in its influence.

Everything that shows up in your life is supposed to. This includes the falls in your life, which provide you with the energy to propel yourself to a higher state of awareness.

Manifesting is a higher state of awareness than merely feeling as if you are being pushed around by the whims of the environment and a boss who is in charge of everything. Each obstacle, however difficult, however imposing, is a test for you to keep your faith and stay with the inner knowing that has banished all doubt.

When things do not appear to be materializing the way you had planned, remind yourself that you are infinitely patient and unattached to any particular schedule. Most of the blessings in your life, and in mine, too, were preceded by some falls that we were not sure we could manage when they happened. But you did, and I did, and I know in my heart that all spiritual advances are generally preceded by a fall of some kind. I tend to view those falls with gratitude rather than dismay.

My knowing about my ability to manifest the essence of my desires is so strong that I can maintain my patience and detachment from how the details show up, even in the face of what might look like insurmountable odds. Remember, there is no timetable when you have infinite patience. There is no failure when you are detached from how it shows up. It works. Know it, and let the universe handle all of the details.

⊙ Release all judgment from your manifestation practice. The universal law is not a dual energy. It does not operate on the same dualism that works here on the earth plane. It does not discriminate or work on a good/bad, right/wrong basis. There is just one energy that permeates all things, and everything is a part of that power. By its very nature, the universal law is in balance, therefore whatever you desire must also be in harmony with the recognition of this divine universal source from which all things receive their life energy.

This requires you to be willing to suspend your inclination to judge that which shows up in your life as right or wrong, good or bad, attractive or unattractive and so on. Your judgments halt the flow of universal energy into your life and put you at odds with that divine power. It is not that you will be punished, it is that your recognition will alter the natural flow of that energy into your life.

Your ability to manifest depends in large part on your own willingness to leave behind the collective unconscious—the collective judgments that make up the totality of human beliefs. The numerous judgments of world belief patterns that you are attached to inhibit your ability to manifest the desires of your heart. Detaching from these beliefs is one of the greatest challenges of your life.

You have to leave this collective unconsciousness by suspending your judgments and all of those beliefs that the collective consciousness holds, and step unflinchingly into the world of the unknown. You will probably experience a sense of loss and perhaps a feeling of loneliness as you make this step out of judgment. The reward is that you will begin to expand your own perceptions and to accept that what others believe are their perceptions. They are not necessarily the facts as you know them. What the collective consciousness believes to be the limits to their abilities you will know as a misperception.

You will not need to be in conflict with this

consciousness because you will have stepped into a higher vibration wherein there are no limits. The physical earth plane has its limits. You, however, are now a resident in the universal intelligence that is responsible for the existence of that physical earth plane. Make this leap by leaving behind all judgments and by becoming totally accepting of all that arrives from that unlimited supply of energy.

It could be a business card that you find while walking on the beach, or it could take the form of a book or a tape recording, or a message that was intended for another but is in your mailbox. These can all be cues. Send away all judgments about how anything arrives in your life and refuse to assume the collective judgments that permeate the beliefs of most of the people you encounter. Harness this universal intelligence by noticing it manifesting regularly, which is, essentially, in every single event in your life.

As you notice what arrives and disappears, try to do it without judgment and with a feeling of total acceptance, leaving your thoughts out of the picture completely. Your mind will want to play the judgment game. Remember, here you are feeling as if what you want to manifest is already in your life. Your mind will not agree with you, and you must learn to suspend your judgments. You might say to yourself, "I am wealthy and happy," and your mind counters with, "You are not." Thus, you have a clash of opposing energies: your desire versus your mind, with all of its judgments and negativity.

This clash is your warning that you are not going to enter the kingdom of manifestation. You do not get to become a manifester until you have thoroughly discarded the negativity that you have inherited from the collective unconscious. You have to enter a new dimension. This is not accomplished by leaving the earth plane, it is an inward journey.

In that inner world, anything that you can imagine is actually a part of you right now. Your proclamation of being wealthy and happy, if taken to that inner nonjudgmental world, will lead you to feel wealthy and happy. This, in turn, will lead you to begin acting in new ways. You will begin to create a new concrete reality of wealth and happiness within yourself as you generate a positive attitude toward all that you encounter. No judgments, simply maintaining an inner feeling of having already manifested whatever it is you desire.

Remember, the universal law is neutral and everywhere, and is unconcerned about whether you receive your heart's desire. Therefore, you must take to the path of manifestation with enthusiasm and a total absence of judgment. You are going to collect that which is already here and belonging to you, with no doubt and only a fierce private determination to receive what you are now totally aligned with in your inner world of nonjudgmental energy. This law does not discrim-

inate. It receives your energy and delivers whatever you put into it. You must trust in this energy
and be totally free of judgment about the method
and timing of the delivery.

Your mind will attempt to use logic, but manifestation is not logical. Your mind will try to
employ negativity by insisting that you are too old,
too stupid or too undeserving; that you never win
anything; that you have wished for things in the
past and been disappointed and there is no reason
for you to expect things to change now. This is the
attachment of the mind and the ego to results and
past history. It is thinking by using a logical set of
beliefs that you have adopted from the collective
tribal consciousness and that you have been conditioned to accept ever since you arrived on this
physical plane. When you receive this kind of
advice from your mind, acknowledge it, thank it
for its input, but then say to yourself, "I refuse to
accept any energy that contradicts the unlimited
power that is within me, and I am moving on with
my manifestation."

The universal law is far more magnanimous
than the mind. Remember, it is unlimited, without boundaries and omnipresent. It exists in a
dimension vaster than the mind. This is why the
mind cannot even comprehend the universal
source of energy. Your mind thinks that it is the
end all of experience and awareness, and you are
using that very same mind to affirm or deny what
exists beyond it. A huge paradox indeed.

But you can begin to trust in what your mind desires by going beyond the mind. Meditation and intuitive feelings are two ways to supersede the mind. The emphasis is on detaching from the collective unconscious beliefs, refusing to judge and patiently allowing the universal source to deliver what you are now totally aligned with in your inner world.

⊙ Learn to relax in peace and knowing. Detaching from the outcome means avoiding the process of rushing and pushing through life. Think of that acorn that has been planted in the ground and is on its way to manifesting an oak tree. Imagine digging up the acorn after three weeks to see how it is doing, and to see if there is anything that you might do to hurry the process along so as to fit your schedule. Obviously, the acorn and the oak would perish as a result of your efforts to rush the process.

The universal intelligence works at its own perfect pace. It will deliver when you are in alignment with the nine principles detailed in this book. The delivery is guaranteed by the absence of doubt that you cultivate, and total trust in the presence of this energy in all things, including that which you are going to attract into your life. The way to patient detachment is to relax, trust, do not push.

The inclination to push and force is your cue that your mind is still doubting and demanding an outcome. Your ability to trust your feelings and to let these feelings, rather than your ego, be the driver in your life is the key to manifesting your heart's desire.

⏲ Use affirmations to keep the energy flowing and to detach from the outcome. The most useful affirmation that I can provide for you in this regard is really quite simple: "I am infinite and universal and I trust in the divine power of the universe, which is also within me." Keep this always available in your consciousness and use it to keep the universal energy flowing into your life. By stating this kind of affirmation daily, you let go of your mind's natural impatience and attachment to results, and you allow the source to flow, unimpeded, into your life.

See your day going well in your own inner chamber of energy and know that the right people will appear to assist you in your manifestation. Be open to your energy and see yourself evolving happily and easily through each experience of the day.

This affirmation, when used in the morning, allows you to go to your center and acknowledge your infinite beauty and your perfect place in all things that are a part of this day. This affirmation will shield you from the negativity that you will be exposed to from the collective unconscious and the beliefs that are no longer a part of your inner world.

☺ ☺ ☺

This concludes the eighth principle for spiritual manifestation. It revolves around transcending your mind and the collective mind that has been with you since your conception. It asks you to be patient when your mind will demand results, and it asks you to let go of your mind's preoccupation with those results and to trust in something your mind cannot see and your body cannot fathom with its limited perceptual means known as the senses. It asks you to let your innermost feelings become the guides in your life, and to trust those guides. It asks, most significantly, that you allow yourself to know and see the infinite white light of the living spirit surrounding and protecting you, and providing for you all that your own inner spirit, as a piece of that infinite universal spirit, can imagine.

Once you perfect that infinite patience you will demonstrate your trust in something other than your own limited body/mind, and you will peacefully allow your desires to manifest in their own good way, in their own good time.

The ninth and final principle of spiritual manifestation involves the need to be eternally grateful, generous and in the service of others.

REACTING TO YOUR MANIFESTATIONS WITH GRATITUDE AND GENEROSITY

—————————— ☉ ☉ ☉ *The Ninth Principle*

The conscious expression of gratitude and generosity is the final principle in this miraculous process of spiritual manifestation. Experiencing an inner sense of gratitude and generosity is the result of being in harmony with all of the other eight principles discussed in this book.

Gratitude is your expression of acknowledging the oneness of the universal energy working in cooperation with your desires.

THE NATURE OF GRATITUDE

The nature of gratitude is the complete and full response of the human heart to everything in the universe. It is an absence of feeling alienated or separate. It represents our full acknowledgment and appreciation of the energy flowing through all things, and brings gifts to us in the form of the fulfillment of our desires.

It recognizes that nothing is to be taken for granted, and, most important, it is an expression of complete, unconditional love in the form of a thank you to the God force that is in all things. It is a way of being one with the God force in full inner serenity. It recognizes that the spirit within ourselves is the same as that which sustains all life on the planet.

Gratitude, then, represents the whole of ourselves. When we feel grateful and give thanks, sending out this kind of loving energy to the world in the same fashion that we did when we were asking for our heart's desire to be manifested, we feel complete. Gratitude allows us to feel more together and more connected to that for which we are grateful. It disallows any feeling of being separate and alienated from God. The nature of gratitude helps dispel the idea that we do not have enough, that we will never have enough, and that we ourselves are not enough.

When your heart is filled with gratitude, it is grateful for everything and cannot focus on what is missing. When your attention is on your scarcity, you are telling the universal spirit that you need more and are not grateful for all that you have. The nature of gratitude is supportive of our fullness and abundance, and acknowledges that we are the recipients of the generosity of others, of life and of the universal spirit.

Gratitude contributes a loving response to the whole of creation and to your relationship with creation. That relationship illustrates for us how interconnected and interdependent everything is, including the manifestations in our lives. When we understand the nature of gratitude, we can more clearly identify those things within ourselves that are obstacles to practicing gratitude.

OBSTACLES TO GRATITUDE

Gratitude is an inner process. It is an attitude of thankfulness even when things do not appear as we would prefer. Rumi wrote, "Don't grieve for what doesn't come. Some things that don't happen keep disasters from happening." Gratitude is a way of experiencing the world with love rather than judgment. The three most common obstacles to an attitude of gratitude originate in your mental processes. They represent a way of thinking that impedes gratitude.

1: *Faultfinding*. No doubt you have heard the phrase "finding fault." But rarely in the same context do you hear the phrase "finding love." The emphasis for the majority of us is on faultfinding rather than on love finding.

You always have the choice to be love finding or faultfinding. The faultfinder focuses on what is wrong and what is missing. That focus shows up as criticism, judgment and anger. The feeling is of being *against* the manifestations that appear in the world rather than being *for* what one receives.

The earlier principles of manifestation explained that it is essential to remember that what we think about is what expands, as is expressed by "As we think, so shall we be." If you are using your mind to think about what is wrong and what is lacking, this is precisely what will manifest for you. Your inner world is the source of what you manifest. Finding fault rather than being grateful and being a love finder guarantees that you will not be able to participate in the co-creation of your life and the fulfillment of your desires.

Faultfinding does not happen because of what you observe in your world. It is the observer located within you that *chooses* a critical or angry point of view.

2: *Complaining*. I have a motto that I have used for many years that is quite simple but is very effective in overcoming this obstacle to an attitude of gratitude: "Don't complain, don't explain!"

The complainer always feels shortchanged and deprived, and consequently becomes envious and bitter toward those who seem to have been blessed with what is missing in his or her own life. The complainer feels isolated and separate from goodness and joyfulness. Because the fullness of life seems to be occurring elsewhere, the complainer is full of ingratitude.

To become adept at manifesting one's desires, it is crucial to have an attitude of unconditional love, allowing you to feel supported and given a gift by life. The inner experience of complaining and feeling deprived leads to being angry at the universal source that seems to have denied you the benefit of its infinite supply. The very attitude of wanting to complain is enough to guarantee that you will continue to feel shortchanged in life. Complaining is an expression of the absence of love in your inner world. When you feel love, there is no room for being upset with God for not delivering your ego's demands.

The ego constantly instructs you to need and want more, and tells you that complaining helps. The problem with this is that the ego is never satisfied. No matter how much you feed the ego, it will give you a new list of demands almost immediately after being satisfied. If you give it alcohol until it buzzes, and sex until it collapses in ecstasy, and drugs until it is flying high, and money and cars and anything else that you can think of, the next morning it will have an even longer list of demands. The ego is never satisfied, and lives with the slogan that more is always better, and if more does not arrive precisely when the ego is feeling the need, then you have every right to complain. This is a huge obstacle to an attitude of gratitude, and an even larger impediment to manifesting the essence of the desires of your heart.

3: *Taking what you have for granted*. Taking things and people in your life for granted drains you of the joy that you could be experiencing if you were feeling grateful. Taking things for granted means going through life unaware of the multitude of gifts that are here in each and every moment.

Think of the activities and experiences that would be missed if they suddenly disappeared, and cultivate an awareness that does not take life for granted. Strive to be alert to being a love finder. Remind yourself that there are no ordinary moments. Kicking a ball around with a child, watching the shape of the clouds in the early morning, hearing the sounds of the seasons, saying good night to a loved one—every single experience of life is an opportunity to experience gratitude or its opposite, a feeling of ennui. It is always a choice.

Sleepwalking through life is a choice to impede the gratitude that is necessary for you to become a manifester. If you take everything for granted with an absence of joy and appreciation, you will never be able to see the clues that are surfacing that will give you the impetus to take action on your desired manifestation. The appearance of the right person or the unexpected gift that may be the beginning of your manifestation will be greeted with a shrug and a disinterest that will prevent you from receiving its blessing. Be awake and fully appreciative of everything and everyone.

Change an attitude of ingratitude by imagining, just for a moment, how empty your life would be without those blessings. Often, we fail to appreciate our loved ones and all of the gifts of the universe until it is too late and they have left our lives. I think of this often in relation to my own children. I know that all too soon they will be gone from our home and living their own lives with their own primary families. I often sit in amazement, feeling how much I love each one of them. Marcelene and I make a habit of putting our arms around them, and just telling them how lucky we are that they are a part of our lives, and how privileged we feel to be their parents.

This act of love discourages us from taking each other for granted. An expression of gratitude toward grandparents, co-workers, spouses and even the pilots flying an airplane you are on is a way out of the ennui trap. Discontinue taking life for granted. Live with an appreciation for life that cultivates gratefulness.

APPRECIATION AND DEPRECIATION

When we depreciate something, we devalue or diminish its worth. We depreciate things or people by expressing disapproval or dislike. When we appreciate something or someone, we give value with approval and praise. When we appreciate things, we mean to increase their worth.

It is impossible to feel grateful for something or someone we do not value. Begin to see things and people as they truly are rather than your assessment of them, which is an inner judgment. Each person is a child of God. See the unfolding of God in each person you meet. Then you are able to appreciate them. When you fail to do this, you depreciate them.

Your experience of misery, emptiness and fear is related to your depreciation of what shows up in your life. Think of everything that you criticize regularly and you will see where you have failed to appreciate. If you find fault with blacks or whites, Muslims or Jews, Iraqis or Americans, the young or the old, what you are doing is devaluing groups of people. The moment you participate in the depreciation process, you block your ability to experience gratitude and, consequently, you obstruct your ability to manifest prosperity, love and joy.

Essentially, the activity of depreciation means that you are not sensing the beauty of life. Rather than reinforcing the misperceptions of your ego, become an appreciator and, therefore, a manifester by seeing the Christ shining back at you in the other person or groups of people.

CULTIVATING AN ATTITUDE OF GRATITUDE

Below are some suggestions for activating the practice of gratitude. Make the shift to being grateful for all that you are, and all that you have, and you will facilitate your ability to manifest into your life the essence of all that you desire.

⊙ Develop an awareness of yourself as a recipient rather than as a victim. Virtually everything that you possess in your life is because of the efforts of others. Your furniture, automobile, home, clothes, gardens, yes, even your own body are all, in some way, gifts from others. Without those efforts of thousands and thousands of people all working in harmony, you would have nothing showing up in your life.

Even if you are a "self-made person," you could not have gone past the first moment of your independence without the gifts of the very basics that you used to become self-made in the first place. Just remind yourself of this fact each day and gratitude will begin replacing cynicism.

⊙ Practice a silent expression of gratitude when you start to see your desires manifesting from the universal source. A very private, simple, "Thank you, God, I see you working in my life and I acknowledge with love my appreciation for all that you bring to me" is all that is needed. These private and firm inner reminders to be thankful will keep you from getting blocked by those obstacles you have just read about.

⊙ Become a person who is willing to tell those around you how much you appreciate them. Make a concerted effort to say aloud how much you love your family members without making it a phony ritual. Be willing to say aloud what a lovely home you have and how much you appreciate it, or to express appreciation to someone who does your laundry or cooks a fine meal for you. Do this in a sincere fashion and you will see how quickly this attitude is reciprocated and appreciated.

You can practice this attitude of gratitude with strangers. Do small favors like returning a shopping cart to the store rather than leaving it in the parking lot, or telling a waitress how much you appreciate her kind attention to details. The more you are willing to express gratitude, the more you are cultivating an experience of unconditional love, which, as you know, is the secret to manifesting.

☉ Be thankful and avoid complaining as much as possible. Remember my own personal slogan, "Don't complain, don't explain." Catch yourself as you are about to find fault with someone or some condition. Then, instead, find something to say that reflects a willingness to be a love finder: "They probably haven't been taught how to perform that task properly" rather than "No one can do anything right anymore. I don't know what the world is coming to."

The more you practice not criticizing and not complaining, the more that vacuum within you will fill with love and appreciation. Give yourself a specific period of time to practice avoiding complaining and faultfinding, perhaps thirty days. You will experience the emptying of rancor and complaints from your inner self and the opening to love, appreciation and gratitude. The presence of unconditional love will lead you to the ground of yourself, where manifesting your desires becomes possible.

⊙ Begin and end each day with an expression of gratitude and thanksgiving. Every morning when you awake you have been given the gift of a sunrise and twenty-four hours to live. This is a precious gift. You have the wonderful opportunity to take this day and live joyously, with appreciation for everything that you encounter.

Take in a deep breath and be grateful for this exhilarating experience of breathing in life and love. Similarly, end your day with an expression of love, and a repetition of the word for peace, *Shalom*. That word combines the sounds of manifestation and that which has manifested for you.

⊙ Be aware of the need to be grateful for the suffering and struggles that are part of the fabric of your life. Sometimes it is easy to simply be angry at your suffering rather than to know that it is the catalyst for your searching and awakening.

Your ability to know the power of kindness and love most likely grew out of some darkness and pain in your past. Without those experiences you would still be stuck. Addictions teach the elixir of purity. Anger teaches the ecstasy of love. Ingratitude teaches the need for gratitude. Hoarding teaches the pleasure of giving. Your own pain taught you how to be more present and loving with others.

Your chicken pox taught you how to avoid it later in life, by giving you the opportunity to build up antibodies in your immune system. Life gives exams! Be grateful for those exams rather than critical of them.

☉ Remember, it is the nature of thought to increase. The more your thoughts are centered on what is missing, the more deficient you feel and the more complaints you will utter. Similarly, the more you practice gratitude, the more you are thankful and appreciative of all that life provides and the more you feed your experience of abundance and love. The more you practice it, even in small ways, the more abundant you will feel, and, ultimately, the more you will attract to yourself as well.

One of the things I have been doing for years is giving an expression of thanks to God whenever I find a coin, regardless of its denomination. The coin is a symbol to me of the prosperity that has been put right in my path. I have found that I receive coins almost every single day of my life. A dime here, a penny there, a nickel on the pavement. They show up regularly, almost as a reminder to me of all that has manifested in my life. I simply pick up the coin and say, "Thank you, God. I know you are working in my life and I am grateful for this symbol." Each time I receive a coin in this manner, I am reminded to extend the favor in some form of generosity to others. It is in generosity and service to others that our gratitude will ultimately extend itself.

GENEROSITY AND SERVICE: THE FINAL STEP IN MANIFESTATION

The natural extension of being grateful is the development of a generous heart. Perfect generosity is a willingness to give of yourself and all that you have manifested without any expectation of a return. You may find it paradoxical that the final phase of manifesting your heart's desire is to generously share what you receive and to move your attention away from what you have asked to manifest. However, if you review all of the previous principles of spiritual manifestation, you will see that this is consistent.

Manifesting is about connecting to the universal spirit, which is infinite and abundant in supply. It is not about seeing neediness in yourself, but is rather about feeling complete with that radiant abundance. It is not about craving and demanding. It is concerned with unconditional love and attracting that abundant love to your individual life. As long as you are in your physical body, you will have desires. There is nothing to be ashamed of or feel nonspiritual about. Your body and the physical needs of your material self can and will be met with abundant gifts providing that you follow these nine principles and do not let your ego take back being in charge of your life.

When you feel the presence of that abundance,

your feeling of gratitude will push you in the direction of generosity. It is in the expression of your generosity that you will feel most connected to the unconditional love of the universal spirit. The more you feel a desire to share what you receive unconditionally, the more you will experience it flowing into your life.

GENEROSITY AND SELF-LIBERATION

Generosity is helpful for your own liberation in that it teaches you about the inner quality of letting go. Letting go and releasing your attachments are the most freeing things you can do to liberate yourself from the ego. A need to hang onto the things and money that you receive arises out of an inner sense of incompleteness. Practicing generosity aligns you with your sense of completeness and love.

Generosity for the sake of liberating yourself from your ego extends to more than simply sharing your material possessions. Generosity includes offering kindness, care, love and nurturing where it is needed. Furthermore, the spirit of generosity can and does ultimately relate to how we treat ourselves. If you have a generous heart that has no qualms about giving, you will treat yourself lovingly and will nurture yourself without feeling any sense of guilt.

When you can give freely, as an unconditional act of love, with no expectations, you experience what I call total freedom. You relinquish the hold of your self-absorbed ego, which encourages you to believe in limitation and competition. This ability to give without conditions is also an acknowledgment that whatever has manifested into your life has come from an infinite supply and that you can never experience a scarcity consciousness because you know that you are a part of the infinite supply.

GIVING AND RECEIVING:
THE WAY THE UNIVERSE WORKS

Every single time that you take in a breath and then exhale, you are engaged in a process of giving and receiving that is vital to the material and spiritual world. With each inhalation you take in the oxygen and nitrogen that you must have in order to exist, and with each exhalation you send back the carbon dioxide that supplies the entire plant world. The cycle of generous giving and receiving is exactly the same as the very act of breathing.

Look around you and notice how everything in our universe is a result of giving and receiving. The entire food chain represents a giving of life and a taking of life, and then a giving back in an endless cycle of material manifestation. The worms that the bird eats, and the droppings from the bird, and the eating of the bird, and the recycling of the meat of the bird, and on and on it goes.

There is no place for any of it to go other than here in this universe. It does not leave and then reenter. It is all simply a process of giving and receiving different forms of energy. The iron in your bloodstream is a part of the finite supply of iron that will return in another form after your departure from the physical world, perhaps in the wings of a bat. You give of your iron supply and you take from the same supply. Giving and receiving are a natural function of life.

The natural flow of giving and receiving can be stopped by stinginess and hoarding. The process works in the same way on the spiritual level. You send out love and kindness and it returns to you tenfold. The old saying, "What goes around, comes around," is much more than a pithy homily. It is a fact of the universe at all levels of awareness. In fact, it is what this whole business of manifesting is all about.

You put out loving energy to connect to that which you desire and it returns to you. It is a giving and receiving action. You can, however, interfere with this natural progression of give and take by selfishly hanging onto that which manifests in your material world, and stopping the flow of energy that brings abundance. This scarcity consciousness is the work of the ego, which always feels incomplete because it is convinced that it is separate from God.

CULTIVATING AN ATTITUDE OF GENEROSITY

Here are a few suggestions for putting generosity into your manifestation practice to keep the natural flow of giving and receiving moving in your life.

- ☉ Recognize that this is a way of being that definitely can be developed. You may have convinced yourself that giving is impossible because you have too little for yourself. If you are not generous when it is difficult, you will not be generous when it is easy. Generosity is a function of the heart, not the wallet.

You can give of yourself, you can share what little you do have with those who are needier, you can tithe to those who provide you with spiritual food and ask nothing in return. A generous heart is one that places no limitations on its ability to be generous with others and does not do it for reward or recognition. You can cultivate this attitude of generosity and practice by sending love and kindness as frequently as possible each day. It will ultimately become infectious and will lead to more of your heart's desires manifesting.

⊙ Think of the myriad things that you do each day for others, including animals and the environment you are a part of, as ways of practicing generosity. Talking to a lonely neighbor, feeding a stray cat, opening a door, anonymously paying the toll for the car behind you, picking up your children from a lesson, vacuuming the carpet, filling the gas tank for your spouse's car or whatever may occur in the thousands of actions you undertake each day. Remind yourself that you are practicing generosity rather than feeling ignored or unappreciated.

Most important, remember that to give without expectation of an acknowledgment is truly the work of your higher self. The ego needs and demands credit as often as possible, and with a great deal of fanfare as well. Keep your generosity practices private, without needing to boast about your great generous spirit.

⊙ Become aware of the internal resistances that arise within you when you have an impulse to give. Your fear of not having enough for yourself and your family, your doubts about whether others are truly needy, your self-consciousness or embarrassment, the fact that others won't appreciate it anyway or perhaps will only ask for more are impulses that you need to honor as valid. All of these inner doubts and fears should be examined without judgment. They all represent a part of your own conditioned response to generosity.

When you give for the sake of having a generous spirit and extending love, and for no other reason, then those inner doubts will fade away. I am often criticized when I give money on the street to an obvious drug addict. When my critic says, "They are only going to buy more drugs with that money," my response is, "What they do with the money has nothing to do with why I gave them the money. This one human being connecting to another in a spirit of love might be that single act of kindness and generosity that will bring them closer to God, where genuine healing takes place."

- Give yourself designated times and periods of time to practice being generous, particularly in offering service or in giving of your time.

I sometimes notice my young son out playing soccer by himself, kicking the ball and wishing in his heart that he had someone to play with. I remind myself to forget about the zillion things that I have to do, my state of fatigue, my desire to watch a video or whatever, and I designate the next several hours to simply sharing my time with him. It is not because I am so magnanimous but because it is my opportunity to practice being generous with my time and my love. It also provides me with the glorious opportunity to do something I really love, which is to be with my boy, whom I love dearly.

- Practice being able to receive. Accept help when others offer it. Allow others to do for you without feeling embarrassed or without feeling that your independence is threatened. Remember that giving and receiving are the natural interplay of the energy of the universe. It is the very source of your manifestation practice.

If you turn off the receiving side, you cut the natural flow of energy just as if you turned off the giving side. Practice saying "Thank you, I appreciate your help" even if your independent ego says "I didn't really need it." Receiving is very much a component of the spiritual practice of manifestation, and you can work at allowing this into your life with gratitude and love.

① Catch yourself at the specific moment of your scarcity consciousness and use this moment to work on your new generosity. When you are perceiving scarcity, your immediate inclination is to hoard, but following through by hoarding only amplifies the effects of your feeling stingy and fearful.

This might involve something as simple as tipping beyond what is expected, or it might involve extending love or a compliment to those on whom you practice your scarcity behavior. In these moments, work on your highest self, which wants you to experience joy and peace and extend a bit of unaccustomed generosity. Remind yourself that a generous spirit infuses the mind with joy and strength. This is precisely how you will feel when you have overcome your conditioned response of hoarding and stinginess.

② Practice giving just a bit more than you think you can, and a bit more than your own comfort level allows. Increase your patience with a child, hold your spouse in a passionate embrace for just a bit longer than a superficial squeeze, give an extra dollar or two to the maid who took care of you during your hotel visit.

Whatever you have convinced yourself is the limit of your generosity, try going beyond it, knowing full well that it is not going to cause any great hardship in your life. Know, too, that it will give you that sense of spiritual fulfillment that makes you feel more Godlike and which is actually putting you in touch with your highest self.

You can practice a little bit more generosity with yourself than you are normally accustomed to. Order the item on the menu that costs a bit more, or give yourself a few extra days on your vacation trip, or allow yourself the luxury of a body massage or a facial.

EXTENDING YOUR GENEROSITY INTO SERVICE AS A WAY OF LIFE

We all live in this world with other people, and our encounters and relationships with them are a central component and influence on ourselves and each other. "Service" is a word that is not commonly thought of as a part of our way of being in ordinary relationships. Service simply cannot be separated from relationships. We will all benefit from making this a conscious activity of our everyday lives in relationship to God, our fellow human beings, our environment and ourselves.

Millions of fibers connect us to our fellow human beings, and our actions connect us via these fibers to all others on our planet. When you cultivate an attitude of gratitude and generosity, you will find yourself wanting to be in the service of others. You will find it natural to extend that which you receive into the service of others as well.

If you receive a great teaching, you will want to teach it to others. If you receive love, you will wish to extend that love unconditionally outward. Your relationships will automatically be felt as gifts for the service of others.

When you contemplate the purpose of your life in the material plane, you will discover that the only thing you can do with this life is to give it away. You cannot hang onto anything in a constantly changing universe. You cannot lay claim to anything. It is all transitory. The only part of you that is permanent is the part that is unchanging, and that is the spiritual essence that resides in an unseen dimension. You will find your purpose and your strength when you see that you are in a relationship with all other living things, and that you are purposeful and peaceful when you serve in some capacity.

The very purpose of manifesting is to serve more fully and to leave ego-dominated self-absorption behind. Your well-being, which is the purpose of your manifesting practice, is genuinely and inextricably connected to the lives and well-being of others. Essentially, your own interests are inseparable from someone else's interests.

It is out of this state of recognizing our fundamental interconnectedness that we realize we are all in a constant state of service to each other. It is this awareness that you want to keep uppermost in your mind as you generate this principle of spiritual manifesting.

Service at its very basic core is an inner choice to offer a helpful and healing attitude to others as well as to ourselves. A natural outgrowth of feeling grateful for our daily life manifestations is experiencing the inclination to be generous. Gratitude, generosity and an awareness of service as our purpose are the fundamental tenets of this last principle.

By turning the purpose of your life into one of service and leaving behind your self-absorption, you discover the irony of manifesting. The more you choose to be of service, the more profoundly you experience unconditional love, and the more you find materializing into your life.

Service is best thought of as a continual focus in your life rather than being limited to certain kinds of giving activities and the sharing in relationships. Service is a state of mind that expresses love rather than fear, and trust rather than distrust. It is focusing on meeting all others as equals with whom we share a spiritual identity. This inner attitude of love reveals itself in action.

When I accept a speaking engagement, I want to be love revealing itself in action, generously sharing what I have been given. I find that when I am about to address a large audience the best way for me to get outside my ego, which is focused on its own rewards, such as applause, making money and receiving awards, is to meditate for an hour before my talk. The mantra I repeat during my meditation is "How may I serve?" Over and over I say these words to myself until they blend into a peaceful inner countenance. When I go on stage to speak, my attention is focused on serving and is not caught by my ego. In this state of mind I enjoy a loving guidance that supports me in serving those who are in the audience.

Service does not require that you become a Mother

Teresa. You serve by suspending your ego and extending the love that now fills that space. It can take a million different forms, but when practiced with authenticity, from the heart, it makes all that has manifested into your life appear worthwhile.

The only problem that you will encounter with a service approach to your life is in attempting to give or serve without love. The moment that you put a condition on your service, or ask something in return, or expect your extension of the offer to serve to be returned with the appropriate thank-you response, you introduce conditional rather than unconditional love. The imposition of the condition makes service empty.

If you are going to serve, ask yourself if you can love the human being you are serving. If you cannot, then do not give lovelessly but simply pass and send them a silent blessing. If you feel someone is panhandling simply out of laziness and work avoidance, and this is your heartfelt feeling, then do not give. Service without love is obligation, and it carries guilt and anger and resentment along with it. Work at being in a state of unconditional love with your service efforts, and when love is not authentically present, acknowledge that as well.

This concludes the ninth principle of spiritual manifesting. Be willing to take all that is attracted to you as a result of your practicing the manifesting principles, and then turn right around and in a spirit of gratitude and generosity devote yourself to an act of service. The more you practice in this light, the more you will see the objects of your desire coming to fruition regularly. There need be no conflict between your spiritual awareness of wanting to serve and the presence of desires within you. As Rumi observed almost a millennium ago, "People who renounce desires often turn, suddenly, into hypocrites!"

You do have desires, both on a material level and in terms of becoming more spiritually loving and generous in the service of others. There need be no conflict.

I want to close this final principle with another observation by Rumi titled "The Servant Who Loved His Prayers." It sums up all that I have written, not only here in this final principle on gratitude, generosity and service, but in this entire book. Read the words carefully, and as you close the book and go to work on your own spiritual manifestation program, reread this passage by Jalaluddin Rumi, who was born in the year 1207 in the Persian Empire in what is now called Afghanistan. It will remind you of your role in all of this, a role that is only limited by the restrictions you place on your spiritual awareness.

The Servant Who Loved His Prayers

At dawn a certain rich man
wanted to go to the steambaths.
He woke his servant, Sunqur,
        "Ho! Get Moving! Get the basin

and the towels and the clay for washing
and let's go to the baths."

Sunqur immediately collected what was needed,
and they set out side by side along the road.

As they passed the mosque, the call to prayer
    sounded.
Sunqur loved his five-times prayer.
    "Please, master,
rest on this bench for a while that I may recite
    sura 98,
which begins,
    'You who treat your slave with kindness.'"

The master sat on the bench outside while
    Sunqur went in.
When prayers were over, and the priest and all
    the worshipers
had left, still Sunqur remained inside. The
    master waited
and waited. Finally he yelled into the mosque,
    "Sunqur,
why don't you come out?"
    "I can't. This clever one
won't let me. Have a little more patience.
I hear you out there."
    Seven times the master waited,
and then shouted. Sunqur's reply was always
    the same,

"Not yet. He won't let me come out yet."
    "But there's no one
in there but you. Everyone else has left.
Who makes you sit still so long?"

"The one who keeps me in here is the one
who keeps you out there.
The same who will not let you in will not let me
    out."

The ocean will not allow its fish out of itself.
Nor does it let land animals in
where the subtle and delicate fish move.

The land creatures lumber along on the ground.
No cleverness can change this. There's only one
opener for the lock of these matters.

Forget your figuring. Forget your self. Listen to
    your Friend.
When you become totally obedient to that one,
you'll be free.

May you always swim in the ocean of abundance
while manifesting your own divine destiny. *Listen to your
friend*.

— ☉ ☉ ☉ *A Summary of the Nine Principles*

I would like you to see all nine principles in the same place so that you can refer to them often as well as see how they comprise a step-by-step program for implementing a spiritual manifestation awareness for yourself. Each principle flows to the next, and if you apply them in this sequential manner, I can guarantee that you will begin to view yourself as an absolute miracle, an individual who is connected to the universal all-pervading spirit in such a firm manner that you know you are a co-creator of your own life and all that is attracted into it.

THE NINE PRINCIPLES

ONE

☉ *Becoming Aware of Your Highest Self*

This awareness helps you to view yourself as more than merely a physical creation, which leads to. . . .

TWO

☉ *Trusting Yourself Is Trusting the Wisdom That Created You*

This principle establishes you as one and the same with the universal God force, which leads to . . .

THREE

☉ *You Are Not an Organism in an Environment: You Are an Environorganism*

This principle establishes that there is no separation between you and anything else outside you in the material world, which leads to . . .

FOUR

☉ *You Can Attract to Yourself What You Desire*

This principle establishes your power to attract that which you are already connected to, which leads to . . .

FIVE

☉ *Honoring Your Worthiness to Receive*

This principle affirms that you are worthy of all that is attracted to your life, which leads to . . .

SIX

☉ *Connecting to the Divine Source with Unconditional Love*

This principle creates an awareness of the significance of accepting your manifestations with absolute love, which leads to . . .

SEVEN

⊙ *Meditating to the Sound of Creation*

This principle gives you the tools for vibrating yourself to the very sounds that are in the world of creation. These are the tools for attracting and manifesting, which lead to . . .

EIGHT

⊙ *Patiently Detach from the Outcome*

This principle emphasizes the need for removing demands and becoming infinitely patient, which leads to . . .

NINE

⊙ *Reacting to Your Manifestations with Gratitude and Generosity*

This principle teaches the value of taming the ego and being thankful and in service to others with your manifestations.